When You Live
with a Messie

Books by Sandra Felton

The Messies Manual
Messies 2
Messie No More
The Messies Superguide
Meditations for Messies
Messies Calendar

When You Live with a Messie

Sandra Felton

Fleming H. Revell
A Division of Baker Book House Co
Grand Rapids, Michigan 49516

Published by Fleming H. Revell
a division of Baker Book House Company
P.O. Box 6287, Grand Rapids, MI 49516-6287

Fifth printing, April 1996

Printed in the United States of America

Library of Congress Cataloging-in-Publication Data

Felton, Sandra.
    When you live with a Messie / Sandra Felton.
        p.   cm.
    Includes bibliographical references.
    ISBN 0-8007-5546-4
    1. House cleaning.   2. Home economics.   I. Title.

TX324.F444   1994

648'.5—dc20   94-17694

Scripture quotations marked NIV are from the HOLY BIBLE, NEW INTER-NATIONAL VERSION ®. NIV ®. Copyright © 1973,1978,1984 by International Bible Society. Used by permission of Zondervan Publishing House. All rights reserved.

Scripture quotations marked KJV are from the King James Version of the Bible.

To Ivan

❧

In memory of Lee,
a belated victim of hurricane Andrew

Contents

Preface

As I was looking through a book I bought at a second-hand bookstore, the following note fell out, apparently from a previous owner to a friend. It parallels my thoughts to you, as you begin to read this book.

Pam,

I truly hope this book can shed some light for you. Seeing some of these things on paper is very powerful. There is some invaluable information on these pages, and there is other stuff that may or may not apply. Just take what makes sense for you.

Relax, put your feet up, and be prepared to enter your own private world.

Diana

Pam was about to enter a new world, a world of choices she did not know existed. And so are you. May I suggest that you read with an open mind—and that you read the whole book before you choose a plan for addressing your problem.

Yes, relax, put your feet up, and be prepared to enter a new world.

Acknowledgments

Special thanks:

To Bill Petersen and Evelyn Bence, who did their very important part in the editing of this book.

To those Messies and MessieMates who have shared themselves with me in their seeking recovery.

To encouragers and listeners, Paula, Sandy, Hilda, Linda, and others.

To those who read and commented on the manuscript, Judith Kolberg and Denslow Brown. Judith coined the word *MessieMate*.

To my mother, who lived with me as a Messie and did it beautifully.

To my family, who endured many years of my messy addiction and loved me anyway.

Chapter 1

We've Got a Problem

If you are reading this book, it's pretty sure that somehow, somewhere, you've gotten hooked up with a Messie and you feel you've had it with the clutter, disorganization, and yes, the *mess*.

Living with a Messie is incredibly difficult. Nobody, except someone who has tried it, can fully appreciate that fact. Living with someone else's disorganization can place the most otherwise congenial relationship under severe strain. Sometimes it may even stress the relationship to the breaking point.

But I can tell you that there is a better alternative than breaking off the relationship. And there is a better alternative than staying in the relationship and being miserable with all the clutter. Yes, there is a better way. You can live with a Messie satisfactorily. Maybe even happily. That's where this book is heading.

But that's not where you are now. Your life may be more like Frank's or Beatrice's.

Frank's Problem—Life with Marsha

Frank and his coworkers are closing their briefcases and getting ready to leave the office and head home. At last! It has been a good——but hard—day. It is time to relax. As Frank looks at the men and women who work with him, he wonders, *What are they going home to?* Then he considers his own situation.

Frank knows what he will find when he gets home. Marsha is a happy sort, imaginative, a good mother. The kids are full of life and reasonably content despite the ups and downs of growing up. These things he prizes. But the part that bothers him is, well, the house.

He knows that the dining room table will be piled high. To eat, they will have to pick up the stacks—papers, shopping bags, books—and deposit them temporarily on the floor. After they eat, they will put them back on the table, or maybe they will just leave them on the floor and start new piles on the table.

The kitchen is in various stages of chaos.

The kids leave their school stuff, their half-finished projects, and their clothes anywhere.

Clean clothes folded, clean clothes not folded, dirty clothes, all are in their own piles waiting for processing. Sometimes the clothes get mixed together before they get processed, whatever that means.

The family room, the bedroom—clutter everywhere.

Frank is under pressure from his parents to do something so their grandchildren will receive a better upbringing. They did not raise their son to live like that. They can't figure out why Marsha wants to.

The dreariness of the whole environment bothers Frank the most. They can't live a normal social life because of the house. He doesn't really ask much. He just wants to go home to an orderly and pleasant spot to relax, to enjoy his family without the distraction of all this clutter. Instead it looks like a war zone of domesticity. It is always in the process of being organized, to hear Marsha talk, but it never gets there. The piles are just in different spots each day when he gets home. He wonders what she does all day while he is at work and the kids are in school. She seems to be always busy, but. . . .

Frank says good-night to his coworkers and is sure they are going home to be replenished and refreshed in their houses. Forcing himself to look on the positives of his life with Marsha, he stuffs down his feelings of disappointment, almost despair, and braces himself to head home and face the onslaught of the house. Maybe tonight will be better. . . .

Beatrice's Problem—Life with Leo

Beatrice works full-time outside the home. She and Leo have raised their children. Now it's just the two of them alone—together—again. Life sure is a lot less stressful than it was when the children were home. Now they can take care of some things that they had only dreamed of doing when they had felt pressed by family responsibility.

But something is not quite right. When the children lived at home, Beatrice understood that it was normal for the house to get cluttered. It surprised her that after they all had moved out, the clutter remained, maybe even got worse. Slowly it dawned on her how very disorganized Leo was. He would start a project and not finish it. I don't

> *Not every disorganized person is a Messie,*
> *just as not everyone who drinks*
> *or even overdrinks is an alcoholic.*

mean he took a long time at it. I mean it just never got finished. For instance, the den molding was never put on. Beatrice finally took it out of the corner of the den and stored it somewhere. When Leo works in the yard, he just stops his work and comes in. He doesn't put the tools away; he leaves them out to rust. Beatrice can never put her hands on a screwdriver or hammer; they're not in the toolbox where they should be. And Leo procrastinates. He makes lists, talks about his lists, sets times to do what is on the lists, but he never follows through. He also saves everything. Why not? They have so much more space now that the children have left home. Leo is indulging in all of the collecting he had to deny himself when they didn't have the room.

Actually, Leo has taken over one of the children's bedrooms as his junk room. Beatrice could handle living with Leo's habit when she could just close the door on that one room, but now Leo has outgrown the room and is using other spots in the house as his overflow.

With the children gone, Leo has taken over as the chief clutterer. As a rule, Beatrice is a laid-back sort. She is flexible and doesn't want to bug Leo, but this is not the preretirement life she was anticipating.

Don't get me wrong; Leo is not a bad guy. He's really sweet in many ways. He has taken over the grocery shopping, and he helps with the laundry. He says he wants things to be easier for her now that she has less family responsibility. He says the right things. He tries to do his part. It's just that his clutter overshadows his good points.

They have been married all these years, and now Beatrice is wondering if a marriage counselor could tell her what to do. How can she handle this? She has talked to Leo—and talked and talked. He is always on the verge of whipping everything into shape just as soon as his schedule eases up. But, of course, it never does.

What Is a Messie?

Marsha and Leo are what I call *Messies.* I coined the term when I identified the problems I saw in myself. I was a Messie—and so was my husband.

How am I defining the term *Messie*? A Messie is a person whose housekeeping falls outside the realm of what is generally considered acceptable in the society in which the house is kept and whose housekeeping habits cause significant problems in the areas of relationships or functions. The messiness is hurting the people who live with and love the Messie.

Remember that not every disorganized person is a Messie, just as not everyone who drinks or even over-drinks is an alcoholic. A lot of people live an organizationally relaxed life. They may entertain happily even when the floor needs vacuuming. When in a hurry, they leave plates on the table after dinner and get to them later. But the situation does not get out of control. These people fall within the normal range of disorganization. There is a difference in degree and intensity between them and a true Messie. True messiness must interfere in some significant way with one's life. As long as no rational person is pained by it and there is no significant problem in functioning, there is no significant problem to be dealt with.

Why Do I Care How They Live?

Hi Sandra!

I met you a couple of years ago (in the airport shuttle) in San Diego when you were going to a NAPO convention.

My brother, Randy, is a major Messie who I have tried to help (to no avail). I gave up a year and a half ago, fearing I was enabling him. . . . Now he seems to have come to the end of his rope. Please send him any help and hope you can.

Thank you and bless you,
Betsy

It is the correct thing, so it seems, to say that each of us is responsible for only our own personal lives. How another person lives is his or her own responsibility, we say. If my husband cannot walk through his study, cannot get close to the bookcase to get a book, and has long since stopped using his desk because it is full of old mail, what is that to me? If Aunt Suzie in New Mexico likes to live with canned goods stacked to the ceiling, laundry draped over the dining room chairs, and magazines galore in unkempt piles all over the floor, why should I care?

There are two reasons I care. First, because I am altruistic. One hopes it is a healthy altruism. When I see people I care about struggling, I would like to make things easier for them.

Frankly, some messiness can threaten life. I am thinking of the woman near us who was burned to death; she could not evacuate her house because of the obstructing clutter. But for the most part, the problem of messiness is not life threatening. It does, however, threaten the lifestyle of the person who has it and the lifestyle of the people around the Messie, which brings me to the second reason I care.

If I have to live with these messes, it drives me crazy. Even if my husband has his own clutter room and does not muddle up the rest of the house, I feel frustrated if he loses his important papers and is grumpy all day because of it. If mutually important papers, such as a will or a deed, get buried in an avalanche in his room, his problem is my problem.

As you already know, it is one thing to know about someone's mess and to see it occasionally when visiting. It is quite another to have to live with it. Then messiness is a family affair, and I have reason to care!

Where Do You Fit?

Those who live with Messies come from many different viewpoints. Some of you who picked up a book with this title are extremely neat by nature. In fact, you are perfectionists extraordinaire and have serious problems of your own in the area of perfectionism. Others of you are plain Joes or Janes who just want a regular life where you can find the socks and have friends over without embarrassment. You may have chosen your life with this Messie—as in marriage—or you may have inherited your mess, if your Messie is a parent or child. Still others of you are recovering Messies who live with more serious Messies who haven't caught your vision for change. Organizationally you are barely able to keep your own head above water, and the Messie you live with keeps pushing you under each time you think you might have a chance to get on top of things.

Let's look at a number of situations in more detail. Where do you fit?

Before we do that, a word is in order about the assumptions of this book. I assume that the reader lives in a situation that, for bad or good, appears to follow the standard pattern—where the woman has the primary responsibility for the house, and she does the lion's share of the work. This is the case in most American households.

Some changes in this pattern are occurring. As the young men who are used to helping their moms get married, they are helping their working wives more than ever before. However, change is slow, and the fact remains statistically that the buck stops at the woman's desk when it comes to housework, no matter how much help she gets.

The purpose of this book is not to crusade for change—to the more traditional ways of full-time homemaker wife or to a more egalitarian distribution of housework between working husband and working wife. That issue is outside the scope of this book. The purpose of my writing is to help those of you who live with a Messie no matter what your relationship to that Messie.

Another word—about my use of pronouns. To avoid overusing the awkward he or she construction, I alternate pronouns, sometimes using he and sometimes she. For the simple reason that I'm sure most readers of this book will be women who are frustrated with their male Messies, I often refer to the Messie as he.

The Perfectionist Who Lives with a Messie

Superperfectionists try to manipulate their world so they can be in control. They do this by keeping everything in the strictest and most orderly condition. Often they pare down their belongings to a minimum so they can be sure not to lose their grip on the precision required for their comfort. Anything out of place upsets them. Their houses look like model homes.

I know an air force officer who will not allow so much as an unwashed spoon to lie in the sink. This is an affront to his sense of order. The house is not exactly dysfunctional, but he is. His situation is similar to that of a person who, though never overweight, maintains a svelte figure by purging. That person may look all right (until she becomes underweight), but she is not healthy.

Sometimes an average housekeeper finds herself being treated like a Messie simply because she is living with a husband who is a rigid organizer. In such a situation, if the average housekeeper is not careful, she can easily sink into the stress and low self-esteem of a Messie simply because it is imposed upon her by unreasonable expectations. The husband becomes more and more like the boss of the house, and the wife, the full-time hired help.

If the superorganizer is a woman, the husband, pretty orderly by most standards, will find that at home he cannot move without thinking about how what he is doing will fit in with her standards. He either has to become fastidious or find reasons to stay out of the house.

Whether the husband or wife is the superorganizer, the couple might argue a lot. This won't get far usually

> *Do opposites attract? Yes,*
> *but they don't necessarily like what they attract.*

because the perfectionist is really hooked on order and control. He or she becomes upset if challenged and feels that he or she is totally right. Any person who deviates from the standards is wrong and requires correction. The controller has a divine calling to maintain a *House Beautiful* home.

People who go through all the grief of being treated like a Messie when they are not chronically disorganized are not really Messies. I call them pseudo-Messies, but their lives can be as hard as a Messie's. In fact, it could be worse because a Messie can improve her condition, but no matter how hard pseudo-Messies try, they are unlikely to meet the unrealistically high standards of the perfectionists with whom they live.

When Opposites Attract

Do opposites attract? Yes, but they don't necessarily like what they attract. There is much evidence that we choose people as marriage partners or friends who round out our own personalities. In the area of organization (and marriage) it works something like this.

Cleanie Husband and Messie Wife

Bill and Mary meet. They are attracted to each other by the who-knows-what that has caused men and women to fancy each other since Adam met Eve. They decide to size each other up as marriage partners. As they get to know each other, Mary realizes that one of the qualities she values in Bill is his organizational proficiency. He is always on time, pays his bills promptly, keeps a neat car. . . . She could use a little order in her life.

Bill realizes that he has these good qualities, but he also knows that he is a little uptight. He admires Mary's spontaneity. She is more casual. She is sometimes a little late, is a little messy in her house and car. She seems more fun loving than he. He could use a little of that in his life.

For these and many other reasons, Bill and Mary decide to marry. Bill soon has evidence that the "little messy" he had seen earlier was just the tip of the iceberg. While they were dating, Mary had actually worked very hard to make things neat when Bill came over. Before marriage he had seen her at her best.

Now, because she has more responsibility as a married woman, things get worse. Bill becomes frustrated with Mary's housekeeping. He wanted casual; this is chaos. Mary grows frustrated with Bill. She is having a hard enough time trying to keep on top of her new responsibilities in the house. Now to make matters worse, Bill is on her case. She is beginning to see the other side of the picture of Bill's neatness.

Bill and Mary had not fully considered the implications of their differences. Those differences are now very irritating to them both, especially Bill, who has the upper hand in this debate because everyone knows—even Mary agrees—that the house should be neat.

Should Mary and Bill have ever married? Perhaps they should have looked around for someone more compatible with their characteristics. Actually, let me suggest that any reader considering a mate not gloss over this important area. Housekeeping and organization can become a serious and daily point of contention.

However, Bill and Mary, like many of you, are already married. Now they have to work this problem out somehow.

As with Bill and Mary, it is not unusual when it is the wife who is messy and the husband who is neat. Because "everyone knows" the house is primarily the responsibility of the wife, this puts her under tremendous pressure. He is not very happy either—to put it mildly.

Cleanie Wife and Messie Husband

Sometimes the husband is the one who is messy while the wife is organized. She sees the house as her responsibility, but the husband may see it as his domain. She has the responsibility to keep the premises neat, but he has the final word. She has no power to do her job; this is the worst position to be in.

He puts his tools by the front door of the living room. That is where he wants them. They both believe that the husband is the head of the house. Because in their marriage he has the final word, she has no power to move the tools. Then he wants to air out his shirt over the dining room chair and leave his book open on the lamp table in the living room. If he leaves his shoes in the living room and she puts them away in the bedroom closet, he scolds her. He has instructed her to leave his things wherever he puts them. He will take care of them. She even hesitates to pick up his dirty underwear from the bathroom floor; that may be where he wants it to stay.

He is the king in his castle. This is how he likes to live. She agrees that this is "right," though she is far from happy with her life. Actually she is distraught. She tries to tell him, but he doesn't understand. Their life seems fine to him, and that is the way it is left. For now. Eventually something will blow up—probably the wife. Or maybe she will blow him up and his chaotic castle with him. A Cleanie cannot live in a messy house long, no matter what her overall philosophy of marriage.

Some Cleanie wife and Messie husband combinations work in a different way: In this marriage, the Cleanie wife rules. The condition of the house is not negotiable. She does not struggle with the wifely submission issue. She does not struggle with him. She would no more consider living in an unkempt house than she would consider serving spoiled food. He *will* put his clothes in the hamper. From day one, his shoes have a place. He and his wife are young and newly married. He wants to please his new and wonderful bride. He doesn't know what has hit him, but as soon as he started living with his new wife, he, who has always driven his mother crazy by leaving half-eaten food in his room and his books on the dining room table, never even carries food into the bedroom. Without even thinking about it, he puts his shoes in their place. He hardly notices how profoundly he has changed. However, when they go to his mother's house to visit, he reverts to his old sloppy habits. His new wife has never seen him sloppy before. She is amazed. When he thinks about it, he figures that it must be something like this: Sons are messy but husbands are not. Yet you can bet that the children of this marriage will not clutter the house.

How does she do this? Frankly, the influence that truly focused, successful housekeepers can exert on all who enter the house is one of the phenomena of the organized world. In future chapters we will glimpse some aspects of the secret of their success. If we could distill the secret, put it in a bottle, and sell it, we would make millions. I know I could sell gallons to those of you who are reading this book.

There is, of course, the less successful Cleanie wife who struggles with her Messie husband. This combination functions much like the average housekeeper and Messie combination that we will consider next.

Average-Messie Combo: A Recipe for Frustration

How did he get into this? Or why did she not notice how he was before they married?

Consider the scene: The man who never gave a thought to the whole concept of order suddenly finds that a sta-

ble area of life has fallen out from under his feet; he now
has a problem he never even knew existed. His wife is
losing the bills. His clothes are getting lost. The place is
a wreck. He'd be willing to help, but she resists any effort
to make things different.

> *In day-to-day practical living, real romance*
> *involves a bedroom that doesn't look like*
> *an explosion in a laundry factory.*

Or this: The woman who never seriously studied how
to organize the house (she just did what seemed logical
as it needed doing) suddenly finds that doing what comes
naturally isn't working anymore because her Messie husband is sabotaging everything. Sure she knew he was a
little scatterbrained when she married him. That was part
of his charm. She had planned to change him a little, give
a little structure to his life. Women have taken that role
for years. But it hasn't been working, and now his pernicious disorder is out of control.

Alexandra Stoddard is an interior designer who writes
about gracious living and order in one's environment. With
a growing sense of bitterness and loss, the average person
who wakes up living with a Messie might read these words
from Stoddard's book *Living Beautifully Together:*

> The happiest couples are the ones who both share a strong
> love of home. If both people are not equally concerned
> about the way their house or apartment functions, looks,
> and feels, it is usually a danger sign in the relationship. . . .
> Where and how we live gives clues to our relation-
> ships. If a lover is concerned for his love, he will leave
> the bathroom neat and fresh. Lovers think of the other
> person's pleasure and happiness. Tidying up becomes a

love act, a gesture of affection. When you make things nice for a love, it is fun for you. (New York: Doubleday, 1989.)

If it is really true that a lover "concerned for his love . . . will leave the bathroom neat and fresh," what does that say about the Messie husband's love for his wife? What does it say about the love of the average man's wife when she does not seem concerned about how the cluttered house affects him? These questions gnaw at the mind as the years pass by.

A house is just a house. True love is what really matters—or so young, idealistic lovers think. But in day-to-day practical living, real romance involves a bedroom that doesn't look like an explosion in a laundry factory and a life that is free of stress about where the bills are or where the other shoe is.

Two Messies Sharing a House: Recipe for Disaster

Two Messies live together and you have a recipe for disaster. They are at odds with each other, yet their chief enemy is the house. Living together in the disheveled environment makes them both crazy. They blame each other. The wife gets the chief blame, because she is deemed to be in charge of the house. He, bless his soul, had expected her to take care of his organizational needs in her charming, casual, easygoing way. In his careless fashion, he had not exactly noticed before they got married that she was a little deficient in the neatness area. Perhaps she had lived in her mother's house and reaped the benefit of her mom's organizational talents. Perhaps she had lived in a dorm room or a small apartment that she could handle. But now, with the two of them together as Messies, her abilities falter.

Consider the story of Gwendolyn, a self-confessed but recovering Messie:

> I am still having a great deal of difficulty in getting co-operation from my family. I have a wonderful marriage in every other way with my husband, but he has always been a major Messie. Although he cleans very well when he wants to, he does it only to keep other people off his back. He himself cares very little if he has to wade ankle-deep in garbage to get from the sofa to the TV. He tells me he understands my position, promises he will pick up his own messes, and then lets them go until I get so tired of waiting that I do it myself.
>
> He is a wonderful man. He swears that at the time he makes the promise, he means to keep it. But unless I nag and yell, which I don't want to do, he simply doesn't fol-low through with what he has promised. Meanwhile, while I am waiting, the house is a disaster and the peo-ple in our acquaintance assume it is my shortcomings that make it that way. The plain truth is, I have enough trouble trying to reform myself without having to work around him as well.

I've told you that I—a recovering Messie—live with a Messie. We've lived out the recipe for disaster. I don't want to give many details of our story. The group I founded, Messies Anonymous, respects the privacy of its members. For now, just trust me: I know what it's like to live day in and out with a practicing Messie. The suggestions I give to you for working through your problems are field-tested in my own living room, bedroom, and kitchen. They're not working miracles, but slowly, surely, my world and my relationship is changing—for the better.

Seeing the Problem

Since you're reading this book, I assume you see or someone who cares about you sees that you have a problem. Even though you recognize the problem as it relates to the house, you—the MessieMate—may not clearly see that the problem is not basically the house; the problem is the Messie you live with.

Your Messie may not fully appreciate how bad the situation is or how long it has been going on. You can see how much your mate is hurting himself or herself with a chronically disorganized way of life, but he or she doesn't see it the way you do. The one you love may think it is a temporary and controllable condition. You, however, are beginning to see what the Messie cannot—that his or her life is out of control and unmanageable.

You may hint or suggest or yell or give ultimatums. He does not change. He doesn't even plug in to the fact that there is a problem. If he would only listen to you. You could help him so much. Just one or two simple changes on his part would change his life—and yours—for the better.

Sometimes he becomes angry when you challenge him about his disorganization. Sometimes he almost convinces you that it is you who has a problem with being overorganized, uptight.

Sometimes your Messie may try to change for your sake, but it does not last long. On occasion, you actually *show* him how to do things better. Sometimes you even do it for him. It is obvious to you how much better things are when they are done your way. You feel confident that, once he sees how well it works, he will continue with the plan you have set up. What sane person would not? But then, well, you know what happens the second you leave him alone. He abandons your system and everything returns to chaos.

You are at your wit's end. Is he dumb? Is she just stubborn? Doesn't he care about what you want? Perhaps she has an emotional problem? What *is* his problem?

Your questions are healthy. They show that you are realizing that, in the end, it is neither the house nor the mess that is the problem. It is the Messie. If, by some miracle, the house were suddenly fully organized overnight, it would soon be back in the condition it is now, unless the Messie who lives in the house were temperamentally changed. It is not the house that is "sick." It is the Messie.

Messiness is not strictly a disease like measles or cancer. It is not an addiction like alcoholism. But it acts very much like a disease or an addiction in some of its parts. M. Scott Peck in his book *People of the Lie* defines illness and disease as "any defect in the structure of our bodies or our personalities that prevents us from fulfilling our potential as human beings." Using that broad definition, messiness and many other lifestyle disorders can be viewed as a disease.

Some critics state that the disease model causes problems because it can make a sufferer view herself as a victim, helpless in the face of the disorder. They say that the label encourages people to excuse their own behavior and become dependent on a recovery program.

I see it otherwise: The disease model focuses the Messie on the fact that there is a definite problem he is responsible for dealing with. It breaks through denial. Defining and admitting a personal problem is a big breakthrough. You might be very grateful if the Messie you care about would just say, "There is something seriously wrong with me. I don't know what to call it. I don't know how I can help it, but something is very, very wrong."

The word *Messie* gives a name to the problem. That is only the beginning, but it *is* a beginning. This kind of beginning is not easy to get, because it calls for a painful recognition.

Right now, your Messie may be a long way from breaking through his or her denial. But that's not the story with you. You're waking up. You want some answers.

Keep reading—but know that this book is not about miracles. It's about maturing and growing and honesty and love.

Chapter 2
The Mind of the Messie

Dear Sandra,

I really need help bad! You couldn't even believe how much stuff I've gathered in the last ten to fifteen years.

I've reached the point that every time I start cleaning and sorting, I don't know which way to turn. I have mountains of clothes, books, magazines, and tools in several storage houses I bought cheap. I also rented some garages, all to store more stuff. My wife is at the end of her rope and is tired of living in a warehouse.

Please help me save my marriage. I didn't used to be this way. When in my teens everything was orderly. Not till about age thirty did I begin to collect things.

Dad's passed away and Mom is in a nursing home. I have all of my father's things, all my uncle's stuff, and one uncle to go.

I hate to part with anything, but if I don't soon I'll be living in the street. I've collected cars, pickups, bicycles—all to have a sale someday—but I'm running out of room. I guess I'm a compulsive buyer, but I've stopped going to auctions, yard sales, and flea markets.

Please write and maybe you can get me some answers. I keep trying to get rid of stuff, but I didn't realize till just lately what I have because I try and keep busy doing odd jobs so I've really no set schedule.

Your friend (almost divorced)

Looking for Answers

Messies are not dumb. We do what we do for a reason that makes sense at some level. Often we are attempting to meet some need. Sometimes we are acting out some aspect of our lives that is not immediately obvious. Whatever the reason, both you and the Messie know that things are not working out well.

The tendency for both the Messie and the MessieMate is to try to look for causes for the messiness. We think that if we can determine what makes you or me so messy, we could find a cure for it.

> *Things look different from the Messie standpoint than they do from the standpoint of a non-Messie.*

Years ago, medical investigation revealed that iodine deficiencies caused goiters. The cure was simple. Put iodine into the diet. So now our table salt is fortified with iodine, and few people have goiters. (I bet a lot of you don't even know what they are.) Once a cure was known, the solution was straightforward. Messiness is not exactly that way. Knowing the cause of the problem is not terribly important to the solution. Yet my experience tells me that you are wanting to know some causes. What makes him do the things he does? So to put the question behind us before we move forward, let's briefly look at some of the *whys* behind the traits of the chronically messy person.

I don't want to imply that all Messies are alike, yet there is a cluster of thought patterns that many Messies seem to have in common. Often when listening to Messies describe their problems, I feel as though I am listening to a well-worn tape. Though they may be thinking through and voicing their problems for the first time, to me the conversation is a variation of "classic Messie." Since I can here summarize only a few of the major Messie characteristics, I urge you to read my book *Messie No More* if you are interested in understanding more of what might be involved in your Messie's enigmatic behavior.

Remember, things look different from the Messie standpoint than they do from the standpoint of a non-Messie. Though knowing possible reasons won't lead you to a cure, understanding some aspects of the thought processes of the Messie can give you a good foundation from which to launch any change. *On some level, the Messie mind makes sense.*

Trying to Deaden the Pain

It is tempting to suggest that if Messies were in tune with the possibilities for graciousness in their lives, they would not continue in the degrading lifestyle of messiness. It seems logical that a truly genteel person would surround himself with quality living. While this idea makes sense, it does not apply to many who are Messies.

Of course, there are some, as with any part of the population, who simply don't care about quality living. These for one reason or another are uninterested in the finer qualities of life whether they have to do with altruism, the arts, education, environment, relationships, or, as in our case, the house. Their messiness is just a part of their general overall outlook on life. These Messies usually are of the "garden variety"; they clutter up the place without going to extremes. Often, but not always, these are men who have women picking up after them, fussing about it, and keeping them from getting in deep organizational trouble. I've occasionally run into an extreme Messie who convinced me he or she really didn't care about the mess, but that is the exception.

More often we Messies have to deaden certain sensitive parts of our natures in order to keep from going crazy living as we do. You see, people who have lost their vision for the possibilities and graciousness of life are not so jarred by the ugliness of disorder. Being fully aware of how much we are hurting ourselves by maintaining the messy lifestyle would bring us face to face with more pain than we want to confront.

Sometimes fellow Messies who allow themselves to feel their own pain talk to me about their frustrations. They cry and say that they can't go on. But many sweet, creative, and intelligent Messies handle their distress by denying it and the harm it is causing them.

It is hard to live with a Messie. You and I both know how true that is. But it may be even harder to *be* the Messie. Again, I know, because I've been there.

My Story

The things I tell those of you who are not Messies about being a Messie are from a very personal perspective. Perhaps because of what I have suffered, I can help you understand the dynamics of your life with your Messie.

For years my dear husband lived with me in a house of such clutter and chaos that I, and probably he, despaired of ever living in any semblance of normalcy. When I first got married, I almost immediately discovered to my amazement that the little bit of distractibility I had experienced in my earlier years—living in my mother's orderly house or with my roommate in a dorm room—burst into full-blown messiness.

It had never occurred to me that I would have such a problem. I don't recall even knowing anyone who had the problem, although I vaguely remember having read about brothers in New York who had died under the clutter in their home. For years I could hardly perceive that the declining condition of my disheveled house really was a problem. Oh, I knew I had too little time, too little storage, too much stuff, and too many better things to do, but I wouldn't admit I had a chronic problem. For years I thought that the condition of my house was under my control; I could change the house if I ever decided to. I was somewhat like alcoholics who say they can quit any time they want to, but they never want to.

Neither did I quit. I began to isolate myself from people lest they find out my secret. I struggled to put on a good front for special occasions. I snapped at anyone who suggested that maybe the house should be kept just a little better. I lost valuable papers and possessions. I lost bills. I lost shoes, the children's homework, and jewelry. I had no consistent way of remembering appointments, so I missed some. I had no consistent plan of storage. That is not quite true. Actually, I had many plans. I was forever developing a different plan, but I could not remember which was the latest.

Finding the stamp, address, envelope, pen, and stationery all at the same time to write and mail a letter was a nearly impossible dream. Snapshots were scattered in drawers all over the house, as was almost everything I decided to collect. Piles of important things were everywhere. I had duplicates of many of the items that I owned, because I didn't know where the original items were. My life was psychologically in chaos. The clutter outside and inside the drawers and closets reflected it. In short, both I and the house were a mess. Life was exceedingly hard and stressful for me and for my family.

Eventually, after many humiliating incidences and failed attempts to change, Messies, like the alcoholics with whom I have compared us, suspect that the problem is not as easy to solve as we had thought. Later, if we are lucky enough to get past the denial that has blinded us to what is really going on, we see that we have an elephant of a problem in our lives, and we can't get it to move one step toward the door. That's when we are ready for change.

The story of my change and the program that evolved from it is told in more detail in my book *The Messies Manual,* a handbook of sorts for Messies Anonymous support groups and individual messies as well. Suffice it to say, like the alcoholic, I "went on the wagon" and made drastic changes in my lifestyle. I do not want to give the impression that I had no struggles or slips, but the change has continued. Now I am an extremely grateful recovering Messie.

Messiness had become the focal point of my life. Not that I focused on the mess. Usually I tried to ignore it. But the mess focused on me, permeating every aspect of my life. And I could not ignore the damage it was causing. I would have died a very unhappy person if I had lived all of my life in the bondage of that destructive behavior. No one, except a person who has experienced it, can know the relief of being finally free from the tyranny of that way of life. Let me say how grateful to God I am for that deliverance.

Messie Characteristics

Juggling Selective Excellence

As we progress through this chapter on characteristics many Messies have in common, you'll see that each leads to or overlaps with others. In discussing the Messie's pain, we see they often have high ideals. Many are highly educated. They are successful in their careers and other pursuits. Some are interior decorators. Some are attorneys, writers, physicians, or psychologists. They entertain grand ideas and ambition for change in their own lives and in the world. Because their disorder is such a contrast with the usual style of their living, they are confused as to why they have so little control over the ugly

> *Messies walk around with their feet pushing aside clutter and their heads dreaming big, beautiful dreams.*

mess in their lives. They cannot figure out, any more than their suffering families, why they cannot live out their high ideals in the area of their living space.

They *try* to live out their ideals. It is not uncommon to see a Messie whose home is a shambles sincerely attempting to pursue a plan of interior home decoration as though there were no problem. She might be making a craft or carpentry item without realizing that there is no place to put it. Even if there is a place, her project is the least of her household needs; it just adds to the clutter. Or she might be attending a conference on improving her marriage, never realizing the negative impact the unkempt house is having on the relationship. She might be reading a book on how to make beautiful holiday memories or vacation memories for the children with no thought of the poor quality of life the disordered house is causing those same children. In short, these Messies seem to be oblivious to what actually is happening in their lives. In a way, the messiness is a blind spot to them.

Messies have this problem because they lack focus. They have pockets of selective excellence. In many things they are great achievers. In others, like the house, they are disasters. The condition of the house is not integrated into their generally high ideals. They walk around with their feet pushing aside clutter and their heads dreaming big, beautiful dreams. There is a sort of disjunction between what they believe and how they act.

That is the confusing and frustrating part of the whole thing both to the Messie and the loved ones. Referring to a Messie you may say, "She seems like such a nice person, but . . ." Then you consider the clutter and wonder how a really nice person could stand to live like that. And all the time, deep down in some unexplained way, unrecognized by the person who is not a Messie, that very clutter is part of the Messie's trying to live a quality life. How or why? Keep reading.

Perfectionism

Messies—perfectionists? I know it is hard to believe, yet perfectionism is a principal interference with the

Messie having an organized and orderly house. Messies fear making mistakes. The worst mistake would be to get rid of something they someday need or they someday discover to be valuable. To guard against making such mistakes, they do not throw away anything. This, of course, is the biggest mistake of all, but try to convince a Messie of that! The Messie has not thrown out anything, but the Messie cannot find anything either. You have no idea how frustrating it is to know that the plan you have to meet your needs is actually the thing that *keeps* you from meeting your needs. That is, the logjam of all the stuff you have lying around (just in case you should need it) keeps you from getting to the one thing you need when you really do need it.

Messies want to have complete knowledge at their fingertips. So they gather printed information in files, folders, magazines, and books. Knowledge is power. Messies also want to remember the past as perfectly as possible. Having rather poor memories (we'll get to that shortly), they take lots of snapshots and bring home lots of souvenirs so they can hold on to the past. In addition, they want to have quick access to things they need—so they leave them sitting out within ready reach.

Messies are also compassionate people. It would hurt them not to be able to meet a need—their own, their family's, or the world's. They do too much and keep too much and keep it too visible in their attempts to meet these needs.

This perfectionism keeps the Messie from accomplishing relatively easy tasks. You see, we are going to perform better than the average person. If we plan to send Christmas cards, we are not just going to address and sign them. No, not us! We will handwrite a personal and thoughtful note on each one. Just as soon as we get the time. Christmases come and Christmases go. We have the cards, specially selected for their depth and meaning-fulness. But over the second or third muggy summer, the envelope flaps stick down to the envelopes. We never send them. We misplace the cards among the debris.

There is a certain pleasure in knowing we did not do a slipshod job. If we had ever done it, it would have been wonderful! Multiply this story by task after task, perfectly planned and never done, and you have a house cluttered with the junk of good intentions.

Perfectionism is a reflection of a control issue. Messies are afraid (we'll get to that too) of losing control. They hope by having all this stuff, they will be more in control. Of course, it doesn't work that way. They lose control and meet fewer needs by this way of life.

Fear

Messies spend much of their lives in a state of low-grade fear. This is another facet of perfectionism. They fear not having enough for themselves or their loved ones or neighbors or, for that matter, any stranger who should

> *Messiness is often confusing because of the opposites that seem to exist side by side in the Messie personality.*

come to the door and ask for some rare item that they have saved from eons past for just such an occasion as this. Messies have a strong need to take care of themselves and others. They end up neglecting themselves, and others too. But the original plan was to keep stuff so they would not be in need.

Collector Messies envision themselves as wealthy beyond words because they have things that money can't buy: One-of-a-kind items. Maybe-it-will-be-a-collector's-piece-one-day items. I-know-it's-broken-but-it-is-too-beautiful-to-throw-out items. It all seems so grand and reasonable at the start. But the eventual reality is that the Messies are living in ugliness and disorder while all these riches gather dust and mold. Yet they still fear to throw things out. The day after they do, they are—or someone else is—sure to need it.

In extreme cases the fear can become what is called an obsessive-compulsive disorder (OCD). In his helpful book *Getting Control,* Lee Baer describes the hoarding-collecting compulsion as "Saving old newspapers, notes, cans, paper towels, wrappers, and empty bottles for fear that if you throw them away you may one day need them; picking up useless objects from the street or from garbage cans."

Many Messies may be undiagnosed OCD sufferers. A deep fear compels them to gather stuff and keep it forever. No amount of reason or assistance will pry their possessions away. You can try to shame them or bribe them. You can hire a maid or a professional organizer. None of these things will move them.

Today there is much help available to the Messie with OCD, including medication and behavioral therapy.

Switching Gears under Pressure

Messiness is often confusing because of the opposites that seem to exist side by side in the Messie personality. This is the case with what I will call global-specific thinking. It works this way:

The Messie personality usually wants to do only big jobs. This is related to their perfectionistic thinking. They take a global view of how to do the work. For example, if a small area of the rug needs vacuuming, the Messie wants to wait until he has time to vacuum the whole rug before attending to it. Perhaps he would like to wait till he has time to vacuum the whole house at once. Or a Messie might need or even want to fold the dried clothes. But one basket is hardly worth worrying about. She will wait until all the wash is done and then fold everything at one time. Or a Messie might not wipe up well in the kitchen after meals. She will wait until she has time to wash the cabinets thoroughly. The lawn needs edging, but the job is put off until there is time to do the total yard, including hiring a truck to haul away debris behind the garage.

It all seems very sensible and efficient, but it just doesn't work. The Messie never has time for the big job. In the meantime, to use the examples given, the rug has a dirty spot, the clothes are in the basket unfolded, the cabinets are sticky, and the lawn needs edging. When not under pressure, this is the way the Messie tends to operate.

But if the Messie comes under pressure, a change occurs. The Messie goes to the opposite extreme and thinks very specifically. If, for instance, Mother-in-Law is expected as a house guest, the Messie turns to minutia while getting ready. Every detail becomes important.

> *Messies may not want to put things away because they're afraid they will forget where they put them.*

The Messie washes the baseboards of the living room, paints the trim under the kitchen cabinet, cleans the rims of the catsup bottles, changes the shower curtain, and fertilizes the yard. None of these makes a significant impact on the general appearance of the house, which may remain in a shambles while the Messie pursues these unimportant details. Under pressure, the Messie tends to become very specific and detail oriented.

The Messie can use this tendency to become tuned in to detail to attack you when you mention disorderly habits. The Messie may have left a huge mess for days in the middle of the living room. Finally you speak about it in very clear terms. The reaction? "Well, you aren't so perfect yourself. Have you looked at the fuse box lately? No! Well, maybe you should, Miss High-and-Mighty. There is dust, yes, dust on the fuse box. Do you know how dangerous that might be? Many fires have been started from dust on the fuse box. You put our home in jeopardy, and you have the nerve to talk to me about working on my motorcycle in the living room. . . ."

This line of attack is hard to counter because it makes so little sense. But it is not entirely a put-on by the Messie, who really does think this way under pressure.

Successful housekeepers avoid extreme global or specific thought patterns. They keep up with the little jobs as they work toward their larger goals. They are able to integrate the little stuff into the flow of the overall. They are able to ignore the insignificant when it is appropriate to major on the major. But the Messie lacks this ability to integrate the global and specific.

Poor Memory

One of the most troublesome and difficult problems for a Messie is having a poor memory. Messies may not want to put things away because they're afraid they will forget where they put them. Poor memory causes Messies to hold back in their activities, professional or social. Because they never know when the memory will falter, they do not take on jobs where their memory might let them down and get them in trouble. They may not want to introduce people for fear of forgetting names. They may forget to thank someone for a gift. They may overlook some important item on their agendas. To minimize public observation of these missteps, they keep a very low profile.

In some cases, a poor memory might be attributed to a psychological condition in which a person sort of cuts out (dissociates) of the conscious flow of life. Such a dissociative disorder has its roots in childhood trauma in which the child did not have the tools necessary to face life stresses. It can be a useful and appropriate coping device for a child when no other help is available. As adults, some who learned to cope this way in childhood continue to cut out even when it is not necessary or useful to them. Adults might inexplicably forget to do something or forget that they have done something that a person would ordinarily remember.

At this point every forgetful person is going to make a self-diagnosis. "I must have a dissociative disorder." Hold on. A broad range of forgetfulness has nothing to do with dissociation. The only purpose for mentioning it is that if a person keeps cutting out mentally for a while without realizing it, when this person shifts back, he or she is not fully aware of what he or she did while in this other mode. A Messie may organize a file or put something up and later may be unable to retrieve whatever she filed or exactly remember the filing system set up. Shortly after putting something away, she may not know where it is.

There are many successfully functioning, responsible, and fruitful people with dissociative disorders. They just keep bumping into these peculiar glitches in their memories. It can definitely cause confusion in living.

Sentimentality

This object is my past in concrete form, the Messie thinks subconsciously. The past is important, therefore this is important. If this goes, the memory goes. If I can't really remember it vividly, what good was it to have done it in the first place? Throwing out something from the past shows my life has been worthless. This line of thinking can also be connected to an unrealistic anthropomorphism—the feeling that inert items have some kind of life within them. Children's stories, such as *The Velveteen Rabbit,* encourage these ideas, and some adults never outgrow them.

Distractibility

Messies often find it hard to concentrate on the job at hand. Undoubtedly the *Messie No More* chapter that has rung a bell in the minds of more Messies than any other is the one on ADD—attention deficit disorder. The following letter might help you understand the problem of one Messie. Although she was never officially diagnosed with ADD, she certainly exhibits distractibility and several other characteristics that play havoc with her organizational skills. I am including this letter so you will be informed about distractibility and its effect on organization, but also so you will catch a glimpse of the inside perspective of what life is like for some Messies.

> My whole life I've been a messy. I don't mean clutter here and there—I mean disaster! I've grown up hearing I'm so lazy and stupid. I believe it. I've tried hard, but my mind just *shuts off* when I try to focus.
> As a little girl I was constantly picked on by teachers for "daydreaming" and appearing "bored" and "zombie like." When I received these reports, my father would hit

me and remind me of how all I needed was more discipline. My grades have always been below my parents' expectations of me—even though I swore to them I was trying my hardest.

My brother has a learning disability. I can't remember the name of it—but when I was reading your book *Messie No More,* I started reading the section on ADD, and I burst into tears. Word for word it described me. I thought, maybe I'm not losing my mind!

Now as an adult and a wife with one child (I'm 27 years old) I *still* struggle with these problems. I fear I won't outgrow them. I went to pick up my husband at work, and it took 15 minutes before I realized I passed it up.

As soon as I feed my son and put him down for a nap, I lay down and cry myself to sleep. Every day I do this—haunted by guilt feelings of laziness. I get up and try to do something. I do one thing and my mind turns off. It's just the only way I can explain it. If it's not an attention span disability then I'm just plain insane—that's all there is to it.

I don't want this letter to come across as a pity party—it's more of a desperate cry for help. One last time.

While it is certainly true that the daydreaming she describes could have another source, such as petit mal seizures, the picture does look very much like ADD, and the writer of this letter would do herself a favor to pursue that possibility with a psychologist. Only a professional can diagnose ADD. It may well be a factor in the scatterbrain-type behavior seen in some disorganized people.

Being Visually Tuned Out

Messies are not as visually astute as their neater friends. This can also be the result of a certain type of attention deficit. On the other hand, neat-nik fanatics are frequently overly tuned in visually to their physical surroundings. I was recently in a schoolroom I visit often, and I saw a new teacher spraying and wiping the book-

Some Messies are able to stand living with the clutter around them because they don't see that it's as bad as it is.

shelves, desks, and sills. I thought the room looked fine. When I asked her about it, she said she thought the room was filthy. She shuddered and uttered an "ugh." She continued by explaining that she was having to use hand cream because of the dirt. (I could not figure out exactly why hand cream was important, but maybe you can.)

I tell this story to show how poorly I function visually. I had been unaware of the dirt. Worse yet, I am now unable to see that the room is cleaner. I do not have poor eyesight, but I might as well have for all the good my vision does me.

Some Messies are able to stand living with the clutter around them because they don't see that it's as bad as it is. This can be one reason why Messies have such a hard time cleaning up. They don't focus visually on what needs to be done.

Being Intuitive and Right-Brained

Much has been said in recent times about the right- and left-brain modes of thinking. Of course, everyone relies to some extent on both sides of the brain. But some people rely more heavily on one side than the other. People who are right-brained tend to think more holistically and globally. They tend to be more intuitive than logical. Research suggests some link between right-brain dominance and creativity and intellectual giftedness. People who are left-brained think more sequentially and logically. (See my book *The Messies Superguide* for more on this subject.)

Nobody knows for sure how strong the link is between messiness and right-brain dominance. There needs to be more research on the subject. However, at this point there is much to suggest that some Messies might come by their disorganization naturally.

Believing in Magic

There is a powerful component in the thinking of Messies that I am going to call a belief in magic. They would never look at it this way, but many Messies carry a deep-seated idea that somebody else is responsible for their lives.

I always loved the story of the shoemaker and the elves—creatures who came stealthily at night and made the shoes. Cinderella had a fairy godmother who saved her from a world of disorder and grime. In storybooks, fairies and elves were always arriving on the scene to solve the problems of heroes and heroines. Somehow I got the idea, perhaps from these stories or perhaps from my own heart, that it was better to wait for someone else to take care of me than to do it myself. I think I even transferred that kind of thinking to my view of how God works in my life. I would be the princess, he would be the Good Fairy, and everything would turn out okay. Thankfully, the grace of God is always at work in our lives, but this does not absolve us of our part in his plan for us. The crippling idea that someone else will pick up the pieces that I drop removes me from taking responsibility for my own life. It turns my attention to manipulating others to take care of me.

As for myself, after a few disappointments, I pulled back my expectations in life. I was satisfied with less. Junk was good enough for me. Leftovers were fine. Finding some cast-off was a treasure, and I was grateful. I looked on happenstance as destiny. Somehow the universe was sending things my way, and I was willing, even obligated, to accept what was offered. When I finally realized how badly the magic was working, I was left living in a sea of clutter and cast-offs.

I made myself deliberately dependent. Then I would not be responsible. I would not plan my time. I waited for things to happen to me haphazardly rather than making them happen in some meaningful way. I did not like to plan ahead. I liked not knowing what was happening. Not planning my agenda relieved me of making mistakes in scheduling. (There's fear and perfectionism again.) I did not have to feel the consequences of my actions, because I had made no moves. I felt that my way of life was somehow superior, because I was in some magical flow. I was also unproductive.

I went around in a self-induced fog, smiling a faint and ethereal smile. This pink fog is one reason it is so hard to get through to Messies. They are not actually in the here and now. Their rubber does not quite meet the road. They are listening to you, but they know deep down in their hearts that someone else or something else is really responsible for any changes you are asking them to make. So they discount what you say, quietly of course, and perhaps without being aware of what they're doing. They nod, agree, maybe even make some effort, and hope for intervention from some nameless source.

In my Messie state, I appeared to be functioning. I was intelligent. I acted more or less as though I knew what was going on. I was responsible in some ways, but in others I was unwilling to give up my dependence. To let go of my dependence would have meant I had to leave the final portal of childhood and enter the world of the adult. That would have meant I had to face the consequences of my actions and admit to myself that the house was the way it was because I made it that way. The house would be different only if I changed it. Life could get complicated. If I could take charge of the house and face my responsibilities there, who knows what other adult responsibilities I would have to face. I might have to face health issues and take responsibility for those. I would have to think about money problems. And what about relationships? Or job issues? It would be asking a lot for me to shift over to the responsible mode of life. It is so much easier to ignore it all, including my responsibilities in the house.

> *Messies are not Messies*
> *because they want to be.*

People who do what I was doing have to spend so much energy maintaining the illusion and the status quo that they do not have any energy left over for really living. Great gobs of effort went into keeping my life on some sort of even keel while keeping up the posture of dependence. I tried to remain dependent and yet hide that dependence from myself. No wonder Messies don't have the energy to see how to organize. No wonder every job looks too big. Everything takes so much effort. We are in conflict with ourselves. We try to blame others, circumstances, and events for our problem. We may complain and ineffectively seek solutions. Anything to keep the focus off of ourselves. Anything to give the illusion of changing without having to do it. But eventually, if health is going to come, the fact must be faced. I am solely responsible for doing whatever it takes to get out of the mess I am in and into an organized and orderly way of life.

Depression

Nothing saps desire, energy, and hope like the ennui of depression. Of course, the less one does, the messier things get. And the messier things get, the more one becomes depressed, and on and on it goes in a downward spiral. I suspect that many Messies are unknowingly suffering mild depression, which is making it difficult for them to function organizationally. They keep trying to whip themselves onward and wonder why it is so very hard to make progress.

To try to organize the house while in the throes of depression is a bit like trying to drive with the emergency brake on. It is possible to make some progress but with difficulty and with a great deal of stress on the car. In a serious depression, it is hard to even try.

Your Response

Perhaps you now have a clearer understanding of how a Messie thinks. I have mentioned these patterns not to discourage you or to make excuses for the Messie. I mentioned them to bring some light into a murky and confusing area. Perhaps your understanding will diffuse some of your deep-rooted emotional responses and frustrations.

Messies are not just obstinate. (That may be a part of anyone's life, Messie or not.) They are not just lazy or dumb. The factors I have described (and others) are definite interferences or obstacles in their paths. Messies are not Messies because they want to be. Usually they are struggling to some degree or another to overcome their problem. Obviously, whatever they are doing is not working. Working faster to do more of the same thing will not make a change in the house. Struggling harder to overcome their messiness is not likely to do much good. Telling a Messie to try harder is a little like telling a person who does not know a foreign language, "If you listen very closely, you will understand it." The try-harder approach seldom works for Messies.

What should be your response? For now, watch and understand. Do not support or excuse a lack of organization. Do not try to manipulate change. Turn your energy into taking care of yourself. Start getting used to the idea that you can't really fix anyone except yourself. As you change yourself, changes are sure to follow in the way the Messie responds to you. Then, and only then, is there a chance the house will change. Until then, the thing is bigger than the both of you.

Chapter 3

Laying the Groundwork
for Change

Nelson's Nest

Nelson was a plumber and a good one. He made sure water and waste flowed well for his customers. But at home Nelson had a logjam that no one, especially he, could break up. Nelson was a collector. *Collector* is a nice word for "pack rat." I don't ordinarily use such a harsh descriptive phrase, because the life of someone like Nelson is harsh enough as it is. I use it only to make sure you understand exactly what I mean. Nelson could not seem to stop bringing stuff home. He got it in junk piles, at garage sales, along the side of the road, from friends who were throwing it out, and in any and every place that a truly alert and dedicated collector could sniff out.

Meg, his wife, was being driven to distraction. She felt powerless. Her only way of coping was to slide into a fairly severe depression. Then the neighbor called the county. The Nelsons were threatened with a heavy fine if they did not get things under control. So, to protect his pocketbook, Nelson bit the bullet and tidied up for the county. Things were better for a while, but now Nelson is falling into another collecting spree, and the yard and house are filling up rapidly. Meg is desperately seeking some sort of help to avert another crisis with the county or the onset of another depression. The living space, the attic, the basement, and the yard are all affected. Nelson doesn't want to hear any complaining about the situation. He just doesn't want to be nagged or reminded. Meg doesn't want to nag. But what can she do?

Messies who are driving crazy the people they live with usually resist the idea that there is a problem, at least a serious one. For the most part, they are not trying very hard to get things organized. The MessieMate thinks that if the Messie would only try, the house would be better. But let's look at another scenario.

Rachel's Resolutions

Rachel could hardly talk as she described her problem. "I am at the end of my rope." (How many times have I heard those words?) "And I don't know what to do. I don't even seem to be able to try. I took a chance and met with a group. These women would talk each week about the changes they had made, but I wasn't doing anything, so I just got more depressed and quit."

She went on to describe how she had moved to a new house. Knowing that she became overwhelmed with too many decisions and too many boxes, she and her husband had kept their apartment for an extra month; that way they could move things slowly to avoid having to deal with too much stuff at once. It worked well until the end when they brought the final loads over in a rush; then Rachel couldn't cope.

Rachel felt she couldn't afford a professional organizer (more about professional organizers in chapter 11). A friend offered to come help her organize, as did her husband, but she turned them both down. The thought of their presence added to her anxiety. She had finally seen a psychiatrist who had treated her for depression but to no avail.

"I belong to a twelve-step group," she continued, "so I know how powerful that approach can be. I feel like an alcoholic who keeps saying he will stop drinking but then goes back to it. I promise my husband I will be better. Then it is just the same." She started to sob.

If you were Rachel's husband, what would you do? Unlike many Messies who defend their lifestyles, who say that they can live any way they want to, and who resent interference, Rachel wants desperately to change but can't seem to find a way that works for her.

Rachel is perhaps the exception. She is a Messie who wants to change, who is coming out of the denial of her situation. She admits she has a problem. In a way, Messies trying desperately to change and failing pose more difficult problems than Messies who are not trying. If they are doing the best they can and not succeeding, then what in the world will help? Obviously, trying harder and making resolutions doesn't necessarily solve the problem, contrary to what Rachel believes.

Is there anything you can do to help these Messies get out of their dilemma which, if you live with them, is also your problem? Is there anything you can do to help yourself? Take heart and, again, keep reading.

You're Frustrated about the Mess? Good!

You have put your foot down repeatedly. You have complained. You have cajoled. You have promised reward. You have threatened. You have used the strong-arm method of verbal ultimatum. You have pleaded. Some-

> *Anger is your spirit's way of alerting you to a problem in your life that has gone unsolved for too long.*

times you have tried to close your eyes to all the confusion and pretend that it doesn't matter. For the sake of peace, you have tried to overlook the problem. You have been as sweet as you know how about it all, and you have been as adamant as possible that you cannot stand this any longer. All this effort on your part has done little or nothing to change the house.

But it has made a change in you—a change for the worse. You have become depressed. So much effort with so little result has lowered your feeling of your own dignity. You have seen your hopes and values destroyed unfairly. You have given up too much of yourself and your inner dream of the lifestyle you wanted for yourself. You feel betrayed. You have given it your best fight and lost. You have suffered as much, or maybe more, than the offending Messie.

So far, the situation looks pretty hopeless. Nothing

could be further from the truth, however. You have a great deal of power to make changes toward the kind of lifestyle you want. There is no reason in the world why you need to continue living in a way that is both humiliating and frustrating to you. But you need to know what is involved and how to go about making those changes effectively.

Where does change start? When your depression turns to frustration, that's a good sign. It means there is some spark of life in you. Are you more than frustrated? Are you angry about the mess? That anger signals that you have a need that is not being met. It is your spirit's way of alerting you to a problem in your life that has gone unsolved for too long.

Are you angry at the Messie? Are you angry with yourself for putting up with it as long as you have? Are you angry at the whole situation and having to deal with it? If you aren't aware of these various aspects of anger, it is probably because stress has numbed you to your own feelings. You have become like a sleepwalker. You doubt your own judgment about how things really are. It would be too painful to think freely or remember clearly. Maybe you don't feel your anger. You just feel depressed. Depression or anger is inevitable when we are not assuming the

> *Your anger will give you the energy you need to make the changes that will need to be made.*

responsibility of taking care of the quality of our own life. Believe me, if you really saw the situation for what it is, you would, and should, be angry.

If you are angry, that is a good beginning. Anger is inevitable when we become aware we have given up too many of our desires, beliefs, dreams, or values for too long a time. It is a signal that too much of your self is being compromised by this way of life. By *self* I mean your personal integrity, the part of you that houses the things that are truly important to your well-being.

You never expected to have to live in clutter. You didn't think you would be assaulted by the appearance of your own living quarters. Your view of yourself is becoming tattered. Your domestic environment is attached to something noble and important in you that is being trampled on a daily basis. You have certain values that are being compromised, and although you have tried to be patient, there are limits as to how long this can be allowed to continue. To make any change, you must be willing to be aware of what's happening. The anger is a part of that awareness. Don't feel guilty about it. Your anger will give you the energy you need to make the changes that will need to be made.

You must use your anger constructively—to your benefit. Spouting off, yelling, or fussing are misuses of anger. This only protects the situation from having to change. *But,* you say, *if I don't, the Messie will "get away" with it.* Not really. The unfortunate way the Messie lives is punishment enough. When you scream at the Messie, you offer relief from the pain of the mess, because the Messie can focus on you and your relationship. If you leave the Messie alone to face the situation, perhaps the mess itself will have a chance to speak.

Think in terms of using the energy from your anger to focus on identifying and meeting your own needs. It can help you get unstuck. Rightly used, it will give you poise you never knew you could muster. It can help you clarify your choices, priorities, and dreams. Most of all, it will help you keep going when you become weary and discouraged. Anger will keep you serious about change.

Like fire, out of control, anger can be destructive. In control, banked, contained, and nurtured, it can provide much-needed warmth and energy. When we manage our anger with dignity and resolve, without bitterness and rancor, others begin to take us seriously.

If you are a woman, as most readers of this book are, you may be very uncomfortable with the idea of allowing yourself to be angry. Men are much more at ease with seeing and experiencing anger. The biblical admonition, "Be ye angry, and sin not" (Eph. 4:26 KJV), tells us that anger is an acceptable feeling, that anger can lead to sin if not properly used, and that it is possible to use anger in an appropriate way.

Have the courage to stay with your anger for a little while. Later it will be appropriate to let it go. But in the beginning of this new venture, anger properly used can be your best ally.

Helping the Messie

Can you reform your Messie? Can you help relieve him from the burden he lives with so that both of you can live freer, more productive, more gracious lives?

Sadly, in some cases you cannot help. However, in other cases, you can be a significant help to the Messie in your life. Perhaps you are a part of his life for just that purpose.

It is important to remember that people are always influencing one another. Sometimes the impression is given that it is impossible to help anyone else do anything or to change. Nothing can be further from the truth. In any relationship each person brings unique qualities that can facilitate the other person's growth and participation in new activities. As the saying goes, that's what friends are for.

You can probably think back to influential people in your life who inspired you to change and guided and instructed you in your journey. Sometimes a Messie benefits significantly by associating with an organized person.

But let's return to the original question. Can you reform your Messie?

The bottom-line answer? No. You cannot reform or fix another person. You cannot make a disorganized person

> *I am assuming that you do not want*
> *to destroy your relationship to reach*
> *your goal of an organized living situation.*

into an organized person any more than you can stop smoking for someone else. Or lose weight for him. Or stop her from drinking. In the end, each person is responsible for himself or herself. Just knowing this will save you a lot of frustration and knocking yourself out with no results.

It is rather like the story of the man who tried to teach a pig to sing. It wasn't a good idea for three reasons: (1) it didn't work, (2) it made the pig mad, and (3) it just made the man look foolish.

What *is* your part then? If you want to help a Messie, you can follow steps designed to influence the most reluctant Messie. These steps will help promote the best atmosphere for the Messie to want to change. I repeat, however, it is always a personal choice on the part of the Messie. No one can guarantee that the Messie will leave the disorderly lifestyle behind. If the Messie doesn't change, are you destined to have your life ruined? Not at all. Can you protect yourself from the assaults on your lifestyle? Yes.

There is one person whom you can help for sure and

that is yourself. You are not responsible for the Messie's lifestyle. You are, however, directly responsible for yours. If you have been living in a way that has been dehumanizing and frustrating for yourself and blaming it on the Messie, think again. Perhaps he will not change his lifestyle, but you can surely change yours. You don't have to continue to live an unsatisfactory and unsatisfying cluttered life just because he does. The hope of this book is that if you follow the steps given, you will have the sane and orderly life you seek whether your Messie changes or not.

Foundational Understandings

In the midst of an upsetting problem, it is easy to forget some foundational points. Let's take a moment to outline some basic understandings important to the rest of this book.

First, let us have an understanding between us that your relationship with the Messie in your life is very important to you. I am assuming that although you would love your Messie to be orderly, you do not want to destroy your relationship to reach your goal of an organized living situation. That would be a poor trade indeed.

I think we will all agree that ultimately people are more important than things and relationships are worth more than an organized house. But it is not that simple. The things in the house and the disorganization are themselves a hindrance to the kind of relationship you wish to have with the Messie in your life. You can expect that when this issue of the house is addressed and dealt with, your relationship with the Messie will improve, as will life for the Messie.

We need to have a second understanding: that the individual Messie is an extremely important person, as we all are. Whatever you do in your effort to solve the problem with the house, remember that the Messie is a person made in the image of God. Whatever you do needs to be done with full respect for your Messie as an individual and with a love that values that person as much as you value yourself. It cannot be otherwise. Jesus said that the second greatest commandment (after loving God) is to love others as we love ourselves (see Matt. 22:39). The apostle John tells us to love not in word only but also in deed (see 1 John 3:18). It is easy to focus so closely on the rightness of our position or on the pain we are suffering that we block out the law of love.

The biblical enjoinder to bear one another's burdens and so fulfill the law of Christ (see Gal. 6:2) gives us no choice but to care about the Messie. As we have opportunity, we should do good to all (see Gal. 6:10).

Let me emphasize that this does not mean we engage in some knee-jerk "helpful" reaction that in reality ends up shaming and nagging the people we say we love. That is not for their good. It does not mean that we accelerate the pleading, nagging, and who knows what all that has not worked in the first place. It does not mean that in martyr fashion we take up responsibilities that rightly belong to the Messie. Covering up the problem so that Messies do not have to be confronted with the result of their own behavior is not for their own good. We have a responsibility to attempt, in love, to find a way genuinely to help the Messie with his problem. To do that we need the wisdom to know what will really be helpful.

We must not overlook the fact that, in the end, we are not given a choice about whether we take care of ourselves. The same Bible passage that tells us to bear another's burdens goes on to say that each of us is to bear his or her own burden (see Gal. 6:5). Overlooking our own unmet needs is not taking proper responsibility for ourselves.

Where Does Change Begin?

The issue is one of responsibility—the ability to meet one's needs in a realistic way that does not interfere with other people's abilities to meet their own needs. It is not hard to see from this definition that Messies are irresponsible because they do not meet their own needs in a realistic way. Some try hard but are unsuccessful because they are not realistic in their efforts to change.

The cluttered condition of their houses grows from how Messies think and feel. It has roots in learned behavior and is often perpetuated in denial of reality. Junk is "my collection." Piles of old papers and articles are "research." This goes on for years, and the Messie will still tell you that the condition of the house is temporary. He will take care of it just as soon as he has the time.

To come closer to home, if you think hard and focus clearly, you may come to the conclusion that you are also behaving irresponsibly if you allow your needs to go unmet in regard to the house. You must change your attitudes, feelings, and ultimately your behavior if your needs are going to be met. Sometimes one must make behavioral changes first in faith that attitude and feeling changes will follow. The excuse that you cannot make changes because the Messie is the source of the problem is just that—an excuse.

Here's the bottom line: If you are hurting because of your lifestyle with a Messie, it is your responsibility to effect the changes necessary.

Perhaps now would be a good time to address the whole concept of change. I want to remind you of what you already know: In your heart you are the final authority on what you should do about your problems. This is the age of self-improvement: Experts enthusiastically suggest, as I myself am suggesting, that help is waiting for you if only you will do x, y, and z. Stop. Read the principles I present—and other self-improvement books—with some suspicion. Go slowly, pray, and think long thoughts before you start to whip yourself or anyone else into shape.

Read the whole book before you stake out a personal plan to tackle your household problem. Perhaps your time to act is now. Perhaps it is not. If you're not ready, know that the ideas you read here will lie somewhere deep within you, ready when the right time comes to use them. On some level you already have some awareness of what is best for you.

Change is not easy. You may resent the fact that you are the one I'm asking to change. It is not *you* who has the problem, you say. Why do you have to make the first move to make things better? Because you are the one in pain. If you were not frustrated, you would not be reading this book. We're not talking about your Messie; we're talking about you and your pain. Your distress, anger, and frustration give you the impetus to begin the process of change.

There's a second reason it might be appropriate for you to make the first step toward change in your household: Maybe, you could have a part in the problem. Messiness, like alcoholism, tends to be a family problem. The whole family system conspires somehow toward its development. Unlikely as it may seem to you, you may inadvertently be contributing to the problem.

Chapter 4

What's in This for Me?

Your life is intertwined with a clutterer, and your life is being adversely affected by it. You hate it, but you may be inadvertently prolonging the messiness. Just as the Messie may have an obsession with the clutter, you may have an obsession with the Messie becoming uncluttered.

Here are some questions to help you tune in to the extent of your involvement.

- Do you supervise the Messie's cleaning up?
- Do you set up lists or schedules of organizing for or with the Messie?

- Do you remind the Messie about his schedule?
- Do you sneak things out the door without her knowing it?
- Do you buy organizational aids, such as file cabinets, in hope that she will use them?
- Do you buy books on organization and leave them around the house for him to read?
- Do you alter your life to the Messie's clutter?
- Do you scold or console the Messie about the condition of the house?
- Are you depressed about the condition of the house?
- Have you begun to give up taking care of yourself?
- Have you curtailed your social life?
- Are you disappointed and angry at the Messie for not doing better?
- Do you alternate between understanding the problem and fuming over it?

Some of these interventions are appropriate. Some are not. But all show how you may have gotten caught up with the Messie in the problem over which you seem

Just as the Messie may have an obsession with the clutter, you may have an obsession with the Messie becoming uncluttered.

powerless. Feeling responsible for something over which you have no control is the ultimate stress situation.

How did you get caught up in such craziness with someone else? It may seem as though you were just unlucky to get involved with a poor housekeeper. But there is probably more to it than that. This kind of problem does not usually come from out of the blue. Whether you know it or not, it may be that you sought out someone who needed your help, someone you could rescue or fix. You may not have known all that would be involved when you did it, but this is where it has led. How did this come about? How did you choose someone who needed so much improving?

Background of the Problem

Your story may be similar to that of many others who find themselves acting as a fixer. If you are trying to act as a fixer now, you probably have been fixing people for a long time, maybe since childhood. Children from families weakened by problems such as serious poverty, desertion, death of a parent, alcoholism, or drug abuse may try to make up for that weakness by adopting a mistaken sense of responsibility. This is often the case also of firstborn children with many siblings. It happens so automatically and so early that it seems natural to take on the role of the fixer as a way of life. It becomes an important part of a child's identity and mission in life. It makes the child feel real, important, even significant. By the time the child becomes an adult, self-esteem is hooked into the ability to help others. If you are a rescuer, you have probably left your own needs behind.

Many giving people extend, sometimes even neglect, themselves for the sake of others. They do a wonderful service. Frequently these people choose helping professions, becoming doctors, nurses, psychologists, social workers, or teachers. We need these folk. Their efforts are appreciated. But there is more to the story than that.

Everybody, not just those in service professions, has a responsibility to help those in need. It is part of being a member of the human family. Sometimes this is a built-in part of life. Certainly it is part of parenthood when a child is sick or the baby needs feeding or even when the young ballplayer needs his family to support him by attending his games. In addition, those who follow the teachings of Jesus, who taught us to serve others, cannot take this responsibility lightly. A problem arises, however, for people who attempt to serve out of a misguided sense of responsibility for rescuing others.

The problem is that they tend to help in inappropriate ways. In order to be healthy, butterflies must emerge from the chrysalis stage by straining, struggling, and pulling free. A bystander is tempted to help by tearing the sacks away, but this interference is a serious mistake. Butterflies need that struggle to strengthen their wings for their coming lives of flight. If you help them, you weaken them, and they will die.

Similarly, many rescuers step in to help other humans in inappropriate ways. To make themselves feel significant, they do for others what the others should be doing for themselves. Without realizing it, rescuers weaken those being rescued. They use others to make themselves feel needed and useful. They don't see that it is disrespectful to step in to help. In reality people can usually make do for themselves or, if not, would be strengthened by the struggle to try. It takes a great deal of wisdom and caring to decide when to let an individual take care of his own needs and when not to. Rescuers, because they automatically choose to help even when it is not appropriate, do not take time to evaluate. For them it is a given to go out there and fix the world, whether or not the world would profit from their brand of fixing.

Those who like to rescue often marry people who are needy so they can help them. Rescuing is very satisfying at first. In her excellent book *Women Who Love Too Much: When You Keep Wishing and Hoping He'll Change,* Robin Norwood suggests that there are no coincidences in relationships. Even if you did not fully realize how messy he was or what it would mean in your life to become involved with a Messie, somehow you chose that kind of person; to do so made some sort of sense to you, given your background. The reason for your choice may have been to take responsibility for changing someone, but it gets frustrating when it doesn't work. The rescuer's well-being is tied up in whether the person being rescued (in our case, the Messie) gets better. When the Messie doesn't get better, the fixer feels like a failure.

Without realizing what is happening, the fixer smolders or lashes out in anger because she feels as if life is out of control. Then, being a nice sort, she feels sorry and apologizes. Conflicting emotions—anger, remorse—go on and on, sometimes for years, until depression and numbness set in.

In addition, all of this being fixed and helped is slowly undermining the Messie's own self-esteem, which is low to begin with. Being rescued fosters a neurotic dependence. As this dependence develops, the Messie resents the helper. If the Messie thinks he can handle it, he may think of leaving the relationship.

There is a further complication in the relationship between a Messie and a fixer. Sometimes the relationship is so dependent on the excitement and drama of the struggle over the clutter that if the Messie were to change overnight into an organized person, the relationship itself would be threatened. Things would be too tame, too boring. The fixer would feel unneeded and unstimulated. If the fixer doesn't begin to address her own unhealthy needs, she may try to find someone else who needs to be rescued. Or she may work to nudge the Messie back into messiness so she can continue to act as the rescuer.

Facing Reality

What does all this mean? It means that mixed in with all the desire to have an orderly home, all the frustration over the Messie's habits, all the embarrassment and confusion, there is also a part of you that benefits from the Messie not changing. In some ways that part of you may actually be working to keep the Messie messy.

As we try to break through various aspects of denial, let's look at a few benefits you may receive from your Messie's disorganization. You say you want things to get better—to change. But are you willing to give up relational patterns and perks such as these?

1. *The Messie's mess may give you a feeling of superiority.* Messiness is so "out there"—visible and undeniable—that it is easy for an organized person to feel supe-

> *Concentrating on others' defects
> can distract us from our inner selves.*

rior to the poor mess maker. Your problems, and we all have them, may be just as or more serious but not so obvious. Actually, your superior attitude may be subtly encouraging the messiness. Subconsciously your Messie may sense that your superior attitude makes you more dependent on him for your sense of well-being. Maybe it's more true than you'd like to admit. If you had to give up your airs, who would you be?

2. *Focusing on the mess may keep you from facing your own shortcomings.* This is a slight variation of the pre-

vious theme. If the Messie makes a turnaround and you stop focusing on the mess, you might have to turn your attention to yourself. The Messie's problem offers a great buffer to protect you from having to face yourself and your own issues of change. If this is the case, you would lose a great deal if the Messie changed. Change would make you decidedly uncomfortable, and you might not know why—at least before reading this paragraph. Not wanting to face your own problems, you might subconsciously encourage the Messie to remain the same. At least the known is comfortable.

3. *If the Messie were to change, you might feel a loss of intimacy in the relationship.* As long as the Messie is faltering, you have a reason to lift the Messie up. The two of you work in a symbiotic way—like a team. If the Messie were to change, you might miss that sense of closeness. Actually, you might have to struggle for a while to find something to talk about or other projects to work on together.

4. *The disorder may give you a feeling of safety because the Messie is dependent on you and could not do without your help.* You pay the bills; you remind him of his duties; you rescue him by helping out when he gets too far behind. If he got well and could make it on his own, maybe he would leave you. The messiness may well ease your anxiety about that.

All the above benefits may have a root in the reality that, for both you and your Messie, the problem of disorder might be distracting you from some other problem in yourself and the relationship. Only you know what those problems might be.

Concentrating on others' defects can distract us from our inner selves. Taking over the responsibility of others can cover our own self-contempt and shame. We can indulge in the illusion that we are not as human as they are; we pretend that we are not as needy as they. We seem so strong. We make an effort at perfection. We are afraid to be spontaneous. We substitute the intensity of our struggle with the Messie for intimacy. (After all, isn't it safer to remain emotionally distant from others?) Eventually we hardly know our own feelings and needs, our strengths and joys. Eventually we lose sight of our real selves. The real us is just about buried in this substitute false self.

By the same token, others are probably unaware of our weaknesses. We look so good, even so superior. We are so busy, such hard workers, possibly even the backbone of any organization we work with. So, like lively zombies with smiles on our faces, we walk through our hollow lives unaware of the losses we are experiencing. It is only these pesky problems like the unrelenting mess in the house that cause us to wonder if something may be wrong. It is like the lump that signals a growing cancer. Thank God for telltale problems.

If you haven't gotten the gist of this chapter, let me make my suggestion clear: If you recognize yourself as a rescuer, give it up. This may be hard to do, because you must act differently than you have ever acted before. You must change your view of what it means to really help, what it means to be a good spouse, parent, child, friend, or roommate. Worse than that, if you change, you lose that part of you that feels significant and fulfilled because you are fixing other people.

Perhaps the most unnerving part of taking the focus off the Messie is taking the opportunity to focus on yourself and your needs. That may suggest other changes. Pretty soon you'll be growing. Growing takes courage.

A warning as you stop rescuing the Messie: Do not go overboard and neglect him, thinking, *Okay for you,*

Buster! You won't change? Well you can just jolly well rot along with your junk. See if I care, you jerk. Perhaps that is a bit strong, but you get the picture. Your positive feelings for the Messie should continue. Closeness is more important than ever as you make this change. Because you are the one initiating change, it is primarily your responsibility to maintain warm emotional contact, to keep the relationship on as much an even keel as you can. You do not want to go from being overinvolved to being distant. The next few chapters will suggest some *do's* and *don'ts* for accomplishing the balance you need to find.

I tell you this so you won't be pulling with one hand and unconsciously pushing with the other and wondering why things aren't changing. I tell you this so that when you begin to change and feel inexplicably uneasy and anxious, you will have a clue as to why that might be going on.

I trust you are catching a vision of what your life can be without this unsatisfying and crazy dance where each of you moves automatically in response to the other and where each tries to control the other. There is no music in this dance, just an unpleasant squawking and sore feet. If from somewhere (perhaps from this book or from somewhere deep in your heart) you hear the strains of a lovely waltz and can catch a glimpse of a lighted veranda and shimmering silk, go to that vision. There is a gracious and beautiful life out there for you, and you are invited. Answer the invitation with a "yes." Then you will begin to feel good about yourself and your life. And guess what? Your Messie will have a chance to feel that too.

Chapter 5
Moving Out of the Status Quo

Mitzi and Roy live together in Altoona, Pennsylvania, in a cluttered two-bedroom home with their six-year-old daughter. (Of course names, places, and details, as always, have been changed.) Mitzi is worried. She has read every book about organizing she can get her hands on—and some on cleaning too. But nothing seems to help. Mitzi is particularly concerned about their daughter, Sondra. How can Mitzi teach her to put her things away when they have been out for years? Mitzi and Roy are not planning to have any more children, but they have kept every toy and all the baby clothes their daughter wore.

Mitzi feels that the house is interfering with her social life as well as her child's upbringing. A neighbor invited Mitzi for lunch. At the neighbor's house Mitzi went on the grand tour and saw the children's rooms, the closets, and all of the marvelously organized corners.

Mitzi returned the invitation. To prepare, she cleaned the public areas and the bathrooms. She closed the bedroom doors. She did not give a tour, grand or otherwise, but she did put on a nice lunch and was very cordial. Mitzi reports that her neighbor has not spoken to her since that day. Mitzi suspects the problem has something to do with the house.

Mitzi and Roy invited relatives over for the holidays. A nephew, in his five-year-old innocence, said, "Your house is messy." This hurt Mitzi's feelings so badly that she wanted to trash the whole meal. Her big event, for which they had extended themselves financially and she had worked so hard, was ruined. Sure, there were spots of clutter here and there that they couldn't take care of in time, but she didn't think it was so noticeable that someone would mention it. He was only five, but it still hurt. Roy, who didn't like entertaining anyway, said that the lesson in this was to never again entertain—and they haven't.

Roy is the messier Messie in the house. He doesn't want to throw anything away. He doesn't want Mitzi to do it either. His only household job is taking out the garbage, and by doing that he can keep track of what is being discarded from the house. He doesn't want Mitzi to put things away. When she tries to, he complains. It makes him nervous, he says. He can't take the strain of living in a neat house where he feels he can't relax.

If she complains about what Roy does, he becomes violent toward her or he takes out his anger by making a bigger mess. Procrastination is an important method of control. So is handling all the money, allowing Mitzi no discretionary funds. Mitzi and Roy haven't been intimate for years. His harshness toward her crushed her tenderness toward him, and both of them have suffered for it.

So it was that when Mitzi looked at her circumstances, she focused on her house and wondered what she could do about it. She wondered if she could find yet another book on housekeeping—not that any of them had worked so far.

What is not obvious to Mitzi is obvious to us. The house is not the real problem here. It is a weak spot that was the first to tear in their strained relationship. Roy could have a real psychological problem. He certainly has a serious spiritual problem. He might have an obsessive-compulsive disorder. One thing is sure: He wants to control Mitzi. The house is a part of that control. When it comes to Mitzi, Roy is very powerful. *And Mitzi lets him get away with it.* She has thought of divorce, but that alternative seems fraught with more problems than her current situation. So she goes on trying to change the house when it is blatantly obvious that she long ago has given up the power to effect any real change. Remember, in this situation the house is just one symptom of a whole failed relationship.

Mitzi is confused. She describes Roy's behavior as "uncooperative." It is a great deal more than that. Roy does not recognize that he is a Messie. He doesn't want to be organized, and he doesn't want Mitzi to be organized either. He is emotional about it even to the point of violence. Before going further, we need to address the issue of Roy's violence. Under no circumstances should she allow that to continue. Whatever it takes to stop it—counseling, leaving, or whatever—should be done. After the violence is addressed, what can a woman do in these very difficult circumstances? Even though it may not be the most important aspect of Mitzi's problem, is there any hope for the house? In short, what should she do? Where should she begin?

Mitzi is not an obvious rescuer. She looks more like a doormat, but like the rescuer, she has made choices that are now influencing her situation. Now she needs to make some choices that respect but yet show some independence from her Messie.

You're Not Sure about Independence?

This is hard for some women to grasp, but we must live a part of our lives by ourselves, alone in an independent way. By independent living I mean that I must take full responsibility for what is rightly my area of care. It comes under the category of the command in Galatians

> *MessieMates often share some underlying beliefs with Messies that a fairy godmother or a troop of elves will come and rescue them.*

that everyone must bear his own burden (see Gal. 6:5). There are some things that no one else can or should do for me.

My relationship to God, for instance, falls firmly in my court. Others can inspire or encourage, but no one can put me into that relationship that only I can seek as I am prompted by God's grace. The development of my own character is also my area of responsibility. The old spiritual says:

> You gotta walk that lonesome valley.
> You gotta walk it by yourself.
> Nobody else can walk it for you.
> You gotta walk it by yourself.

Each of us started out as a child, and each of us has maintained some of those childlike parts in ourselves. That's fine as long as they are the parts that contribute to our lives—the spontaneous, sensitive, fun-loving parts. It is those other childlike parts, which are dependent on someone else to take care of us, that we need to consider changing.

We are grown-up people now. We are no longer dependent on some other person to satisfy our every need. I find that MessieMates often share some underlying beliefs with Messies that a fairy godmother or a troop of elves will come and rescue them. But it's not going to happen.

It will be hard for Mitzi to face the fact that she must not see herself as utterly dependent on Roy. Before Mitzi even thinks about taking any action that might improve the condition of the house, she needs to think of taking small steps that will build a foundation of self-respect from which she can make more courageous moves.

A successful working relationship, which is what Mitzi really desires, is like the two-part invention by Bach in which each hand must do its independent part well for the union of the parts to be a glorious whole. As we reclaim ourselves in a healthy way, we can come back to our relationship able to experience intimacy without loading our love with our own needs and dependencies.

To live responsibly toward Roy, Mitzi needs to have a sense of her own self—as a woman loved by God, as a person worthy of respect. She needs to know her own strengths, weaknesses, boundaries, and responsibilities.

Acting in love takes a great deal of strength. Because too many of us lack this sense of personal wholeness, we allow ourselves to be victimized by the Messie or the messy house. Because of weakness on our own part, many women and men enable the Messie to continue to involve them in the self-destructive patterns. They are not up to the task of setting personal boundaries that would benefit all parties concerned.

But Didn't Jesus Tell Us to Be Servants?

Yes, he did. Jesus also said that he himself did not come to earth to be served but to serve (see Luke 22:26–27). Later, to illustrate the point, he did the menial servant's job of washing his disciples' feet. He said, "You also should wash one another's feet" (John 13:14 NIV).

Think about what this servanthood means. Jesus served out of a sense of strength, not out of weakness. The Gospels frequently describe Jesus as taking time alone, away from his followers, to pray and allow God to renew his inner resources. Read the Gospels and you see Servant Jesus as a person who had a clear idea of who he was and where he was headed.

A servant needs to be healthy. I like to use the illustration of an airplane emergency. At the beginning of every flight an attendant repeats the instructions: Every able-bodied adult should put on his or her own oxygen mask first—because only then do you have the strength to offer help to a child or anyone else who might need your assistance. A selfless here-let-me-help-you attitude is futile when you have no oxygen of your own.

Mitzi is going to be of no help to Roy or to the state of her household if she doesn't start to act out of strength, not weakness.

Small Preliminary Steps of Being Good to Yourself

Mitzi needs to begin to think of turning the tide in the area of caring for herself. These perks might not be related to the house in which she has no control. Perhaps she and a sister could go window shopping. Or she can take time to watch a television program she normally would have omitted. Or she could go for a long walk. Or soak in a warm tub with music in the background. Let's go even further and suggest that she turn out the lights and light a candle in the bathroom while she soaks. She should pause and give herself any such treat. It should be something fun, something just for herself, and something that lasts for at least fifteen minutes. Each situation varies with the person. It is not the specific choice that matters; it is the attitude change that is important.

How will this make her feel? Uncomfortable and maybe guilty. She is so used to doing for others that it feels strange to take time purely and deliberately for herself.

> *Remember that by nature Messies*
> *are afraid of losing control.*

There is more to it of course: This little change is part of a larger process that she is setting in motion. She is beginning to challenge her whole concept of herself. This is scary. If she stops being a totally selfless person, who will she be? What will her relationship be to Roy, who seems to require her to be her old doormat self?

Most frightening of all is the knowledge that taking control of one small part of her own life suggests to her that she can take responsibility for all of it. That idea is disturbing to someone who has given the responsibility for her life to someone else. The implications of making even small changes are tremendous. A little at a time, however, Mitzi begins to consider venturing out of her old and unsatisfactory way of life.

Of course Mitzi is not the only person who needs to take an initial small step toward taking control. Any rescuer or MessieMate can feel so much like a failure and so powerless that she will need great courage to take even this first step toward taking responsibility. When this day arrives, celebrate your success.

You Can Begin to Challenge Control

Remember that by nature most Messies are afraid of losing control. They want to control situations and people. To move anything of theirs would be unthinkable. Sometimes the Messie is overtly controlling, like Roy. Sometimes it is not so obvious.

If your situation is not as difficult as Mitzi's, this next, very basic step to gaining control may seem too minute. But I need to plant this idea for people who feel paralyzed in all aspects of their relationship with the Messie. Before Mitzi can even think of the possibilities of claiming some beauty in her physical environment, she may need to get a taste for challenging control in a very small and nonhousehold-related way.

The following example, involving a desire to buy some bubble bath, introduces some principles we'll cover in later chapters:

Bubble bath is an unnecessary expense and beyond the understanding of most men. Mitzi would like to buy some at the grocery store. Roy may not like it. Remember, he is in charge of the money, and he pays for the groceries. Actually, for our purposes, it would be good if Roy did object. This is a good place to begin to challenge the pattern that has crippled Roy, Mitzi, their relationship, and the house.

How can Mitzi make her change? She does not steal the bubble bath or sneak it into the cart and then whine when Roy tells her at the register that she can't have it. When she and Roy push the grocery cart down an aisle, Mitzi reaches out and puts a small bottle of bubble bath in the cart. If Roy objects, Mitzi answers him with dignity and calmness, "I really want the bubble bath." Then she pushes the cart forward. If Roy objects again and puts the bubble bath back on the shelf, Mitzi calmly reiterates that she wants the bubble bath and asks Roy to put it back in the cart. Notice she does not try to get it off the shelf again herself. She is not about to struggle with him in an arena in which she has no power. Besides, if he put it on the shelf, it is his responsibility to get it off again. If he refuses, she says in a nonblaming and composed way, "I'm really sorry you did that," and goes on. She may feel scared and weak inside. She may cling to the cart as she walks down the aisle. But the worst is over, and she did it.

This is a big change for Mitzi. What appears to be a small conversation is really a giant challenge in a relationship where Mitzi never asked for things for herself or offered any objections to being neglected. Undoubt-

> *It is the nature of life*
> *that nobody will do for you*
> *what only you can do for yourself.*

edly Roy will be uneasy with what has happened, as well he should be. He senses a whole change in attitude. No pleading, whimpering, yelling, pouting, or blaming on

Mitzi's part. He is not pushing her buttons anymore the way he used to. He senses ever so slightly a confidence and assurance he has not seen before. Even in her final comment, "I'm sorry you did that," Mitzi is saying that how she feels is important. In this grocery store in front of the bubble bath, Mitzi took a baby step in gaining an orderly house.

She did not get the bubble bath, but she did get something more important—a small grain of dignity. Later, she can begin to make other choices. She may buy cotton balls to take off her makeup instead of using toilet paper. Her choices will be small and reasonable. Not all will get through the barrier of Roy's disapproval. But whether they do or not, each request made with dignity will strengthen Mitzi for the bigger changes she wants. Those that do get through will be symbols of what can be done.

We are not here blaming Roy for this situation. He should undoubtedly be blamed, but that is not the focus of our consideration. We are focusing on Mitzi's responsibility for her own life. She was the one who let it get to the point it has. She must slowly and carefully begin moving it in another direction. I am not saying this to blame Mitzi either. It is just the nature of life that nobody will do for you what only you can do for yourself.

Words of Caution to Mitzi

A few words of caution are necessary for someone in Mitzi's situation:

1. *The person who feels guilty for doing something nice for herself may neglect or hurt herself in other ways to punish herself.* Try not to do that. As you progress, try to anticipate and deal with the anxiety and guilt within yourself. It is hard to accept that one of the greatest hin-

drances to change is within yourself. What you are doing is not illegal, immoral, or even unethical. If all goes well, the changes you are making will benefit everyone, including you, your Messie, the relationship, and, in the end, the house.

2. *What you are about to do is very powerful.* Even small changes can have a big impact. Changes should be made slowly so that you can evaluate each step and test its effect on your relationship. If you make changes too quickly, you might make yourself anxious and disturb others so much that you will revert to the old pattern just to avoid the discomfort. Or you may unbalance your relationship so much that you may cut off something important that could have been saved if you had been wiser and moved more carefully.

3. *You may, of course, decide to stay the same, to continue to put up with life just as it is.* Be aware of how easy it is to make no change at all—and lose out on the benefits of altering your unsatisfactory lifestyle.

Chapter 6

Changing Your Attitudes, Expectations, and Roles

Focus on Positives and Accept the Messie

There is a temptation to focus just on the negative when you are working on a problem as frustrating and ever present as the problem of someone else's clutter in your home. Even the fact that we call the person a Messie tends to give the idea that this is the primary identifying characteristic of this person's existence. That is not the case. Yes, his disorganization is a big problem. But there are many positive aspects to your relationship with this cluttering person.

Stop for a moment and recall your Messie's good points. A few moments of reflection will undoubtedly bring several to mind. If not, think harder and longer. Even the things that now drive you crazy were probably endearing points at some time in the past when they were not full blown and you did not have to live so closely with them.

Remembering that the messiness is not the whole picture will help you gain some perspective. You will be able to keep some detachment from the problem and be less tempted to jump in there and try to reform the Messie. You can change your own environment, and that's what we're leading up to, but you cannot change another person. The only person who can change the Messie is the Messie— that is, if the Messie wishes to change, which comes down to whether or not he sees change to his own advantage.

Don't Accept the Abuse of Clutter

Accepting the Messie does not mean you have to accept the clutter, even though the clutter is an integral part of who he is. To protect his junk, he will try to convince you that if you love him, you must also love it.

Don't believe it for a minute. There is no law of the universe that says that you must allow yourself to be assaulted in this way. No healthy person would knowingly allow herself to be served spoiled food. Why do we passively allow ourselves to be given a messy house and wonder if it is all right for us to object?

The Messie may be loving to you and may express gratitude that you care for someone so messy. This makes you feel so good. Look at reality! Forcing you to live like this is not loving. If the Messie doesn't see this, I hope that you do.

Somewhere inside you may be feeling sorry for the

Messie. You would feel bad if you matured and he didn't. You think you ought to be in pain because of his problem; it is the way of love. No. His clutter is not your problem. Your problem is getting yourself out of this abusive situation. If anything, the Messie should feel sorry for

> *You want to make enough changes in enough of the house so that living is improved to a satisfactory level of neatness for you.*

you because of how you have been forced to live. (But he probably never thinks of how seriously it affects you, because his self-protective system won't allow it.)

So it is up to you. Get yourself well. Bring the health of your newfound self-esteem and balanced living into your home. That's the best medicine you can offer your Messie and all those along with you who find themselves abused by the house. Your becoming healthy will set the stage for everyone to get well.

Set a Goal for Your Environment

Before we delve deeper into the how-to of making household changes, let's get a handle on what goal you're reaching for. May I propose this: You want to make enough changes in enough of the house so that living is improved to a satisfactory level of neatness for you. If this is your interest, you will want to use this book to develop your goals and a plan to implement them.

As you think about your goal, consider elements of your eventual minimum requirements, your bottom line, the point beyond which you will not go, the arrangement that will make you reasonably content. At what point are you sacrificing too much of yourself for the relationship? At what point are you being "deselfed," losing touch with too many of your values and goals for the house and for yourself?

You might want to consider the following as general possibilities of what you should reasonably expect:

- My desire for a lovely home will be respected even if it is not understood.
- I will be able to enjoy coming home.
- Things that are taken out will be put back.
- Each member of the household will carry his or her own weight in relation to keeping the house orderly.
- I will be able to have friends over unexpectedly without embarrassment.
- I will be treated courteously when I ask pleasantly for reasonable cooperation.
- Someone else's clutter and junk will not intrude in mutually used areas or in my own space.

How to Reach This Goal

We've discussed the need for you to start taking responsibility for your own life. That is crucial to your maturity and health. To reach your goal, however, you need to expect the Messie to take responsibility for his life as well.

Expect the Messie to Be "Normal"

As I said earlier, the causes of the messiness are really not important to the cures. If you don't make it easy to be messy, the Messie can find within himself the motivation to change his habits.

Your attitude toward the Messie can change, so that you expect him to take responsibility. Here's what has probably happened over the years: Slowly, those who live with Messies adjust to the problem. It happens in such small increments that you don't even realize that, little by little, you have accommodated yourself so that the Messie should not be, cannot be, asked to perform in a normal, responsible way. He no longer is expected to

> *Doing things for him is degrading to you and to the Messie.*

carry his own weight regarding the condition of the house. He may be exempt from normal chores. You do the lion's share while he, poor thing who can't take care of himself much less the family, doesn't have to do much. Is it respectful or right to treat him like an imbecile?

You may protect him from the results of his own actions in several ways. For instance, if he loses something, you take over finding it. Why not let him find it himself or let him do without? That's what every normal person has to do. You'll be surprised at how often he can come through and take care of himself when it becomes obvious that you aren't going to do it for him anymore.

One of the most powerful changes you can make is to begin expecting your Messie to live a normal life. With respect for yourself and your Messie, in time you will ask him (not nag him) to do things you were unaware you had taken over yourself or had given to someone else to do because the Messie, poor baby, just couldn't handle regular living.

Doing things for him is degrading to you and to the Messie. How is it disrespectful to the Messie? Think about yourself as an adult—or even when you were an adolescent. There were and are things you want to do for yourself. I want to brush my own teeth, for instance. I generally want to pick out my own clothes. I want to decide whether or not to wear a sweater outside when it is chilly. For the most part, I consider unsolicited help in basic areas of life an intrusion. To be given help after one asks for it is one thing. To be helped because someone else thinks I need it is quite another.

Most Messies feel the same way about being helped. They have a sense of personal dignity. They do not want to be taken care of. But, you say, when you give unsolicited advice to or pick up after the Messie, you're acting in wifely—or Christian—love. Well, you're probably being perceived as a busybody.

I urge you to let the Messie take care of himself, not out of selfishness but out of respect for the individuality of the Messie. To be able to change, you need to raise your esteem of the Messie. He won't come through every time; he may resent your expecting more of him and actually get worse just to show you that he can't handle normal life. Don't buy into this. Respect for yourself and for him demands that you not revert back to pitying him and to treating him like a victim of some incurable disease. Remember that this approach only fosters a neurotic dependence. He may feel comfortable with depending on you like this at first, but in the end he will grow to resent that relationship. Worse still, he will grow to resent you.

Don't Expect a Total Transformation

You can see we're talking about changing the tenor and expectations in the home. As you change your attitude, even though you fully expect the Messie to carry his own weight and be responsible for himself, do not expect a fully transformed person. Even the Messie who most clearly sees his own need to change and who most fully cooperates with the process of change will not necessarily become a well-organized person.

A moment of reflection will remind you of reasons for this. Some causes of messiness, such as forgetfulness, distractibility, and the inability to process things visually, will never fully disappear. They will get better as life becomes more orderly. Without so much clutter around, the organizational process becomes much easier. The Messie can compensate for these weaknesses by keeping calendars and lists or by having workable files or systems. But no matter how much a Messie improves, there will always be disorganizational surprises. No system can fully overcome the tendency to set something down and then not be able to remember where it is. No system can fully compensate for the inability to "see" something right in front of the Messie's eyes.

Wilson is a cooperative Messie who lives with his organized wife, Betty. Although he has many strengths, he explains his weaknesses like this: "There are many qualities I admire that I don't have. I admire entrepreneurship, but I don't have that skill. I admire salesmanship.

*Arguing accomplishes a purpose
for both you and your Messie—
it diverts you from the real issues.*

I don't have that either. I admire organizational skills, but I don't have many of those."

Wilson tries. He cooperates with his wife and appreciates the organization that she brings to his life. His life runs smoothly for the most part. But he doesn't put his pencils back in the drawer of his desk when he is finished. He doesn't notice where things are. Betty jokes that if she wants to hide a present from him, she wraps it and puts it on their dresser, and he never sees it. In a dozen little subtle ways, Wilson falters a little organizationally as he moves through the world. It is nothing serious. It is not even noticeable to the outsider. But Betty notices and has just had to learn to put up with his peculiarities. She would like it if they were not there, but she is not going to make an issue of them. She has her peculiarities too, and Wilson puts up with those.

Perfection is too high a goal. It is unrealistic, and besides, it can backfire and be expected of you.

Relational *Do's* and *Don'ts*

We're leading up to carrying out specific requests for change. Before we present them, let me give you several *do's* and *don'ts* for relating to the Messie.

Don't Argue with the Messie

Arguing accomplishes nothing positive. Save the energy you would expend in arguing and begin putting it toward taking care of yourself. Concentrate on living with the good consequences of your good actions. That is where your focus lies.

Remember, arguing accomplishes a purpose for both you and your Messie—it diverts you from the real issues. Arguing keeps both of you from having to make progress. *But,* you protest, *what can I do? The mess is unbearable.* Hang in there and I will suggest alternatives to arguing. But for right now, remember that arguing is a way of perpetuating the problem. The Messie wants you to argue. It is familiar. It serves the purpose of keeping you stuck. If you should stop arguing, the Messie might try to goad you into fussing about the house again. He might create even greater messes so you will be forced to start yelling at him again. The Messie intuitively knows that arguing gives the illusion of progress—but without real change.

In addition, arguing robs you of the dignity and calm you will need to have any hope of success. It kicks up guilt and remorse that only complicates and hinders progress. It lowers you to a position of frenzied helplessness. Then you are not on a footing for improving your life. So for your own sake, don't resort to arguments.

Don't Nag about the Mess

This *don't* is closely connected to "don't argue." Don't nag. Maybe there has been a crisis. Someone from work dropped by and found the house "like that"—and you were embarrassed. Or maybe something important has been lost in the chaos. Or maybe the chronic frustration of living with clutter has broken through your patience again, and you want to make sure the Messie knows just how serious things are.

Try not to remind the Messie about his failure and your feelings about it. When you accept the reality that you cannot change him, there is no need for fussing. When conditions get to you, and you think you are about to lose it, leave the house or leave the room. Or close your eyes and dream. Or call a supportive friend.

It may seem as if the Messie is getting off scot-free. You reason that it is only right that he should be called into account for his actions. If you don't say anything, you reason, he will think it is okay with you for him to continue. There is a time to say something, but you're not ready yet. There are things that need to be said, but fussing is not the best way to say them. Hold off at this point, and when the appropriate time comes, you will be prepared. Your time will come to state your own values, thoughts, and beliefs in a quiet, nonblaming way with respect for the different ways you and the Messie view things. That kind of statement is appropriate and beneficial.

For his part, the Messie will at first feel relieved not to be fussed at. After a while, he may miss the attention of being the center of your concern. Still later, he may feel decidedly uncomfortable because your different behavior shows a real change is underway in your life. Even later, the discomfort will be because your detachment has taken away the buffer he used to have between himself and his problem. When you leave him to face the junk without the distraction of your involvement, it begins to occur to him that he is responsible for his own recovery. This is an uncomfortable thought indeed.

As I've mentioned, you will be making requests. That's fine, but be careful you don't develop hit-and-run tactics, saying a critical word and then darting out of the conversation. This is not a matter of "read my lips." We want people to read our actions, instead.

Of course, this whole thing can be taken to the extreme of not saying any negative word any time about any thing. That would be unnatural and foolish as well. I suggest you keep a chart of each time you catch yourself being critical. Those silent check marks on a piece of paper have a way of speaking volumes.

Don't Tell Him How to Do It

I've just said you should ask the Messie to do certain cleanup chores, but refrain from giving detailed instructions of how to do it. Again, it will cause resentment and make you look as if you feel superior. That's not what this is about. This isn't about power. It's about responsibility.

There's one scenario where this advice doesn't hold—that's with a Messie who *asks for and is grateful for instructions* because he sincerely wants to reform but simply doesn't know how to go about making a change. I'll talk about such a case later in the book (see p. 152).

Don't Ask Permission to Make Household Changes

It is amazing how much power a Messie can wield in relation to the functioning of the house. He obviously is not able to handle the household organization, and yet in many ways the Messie has the final word as to how things are handled. The Messie needs to feel as if he is in control. Frequently the internal family system is very convoluted. The Messie appears to be in charge, but in reality he is being taken care of.

In many homes, the rescuer is dedicated to meeting the Messie's need to feel in control. To give the Messie what he needs, the rescuer pretends, along with the Messie, that the Messie is a strong, capable provider of what the home needs and that the mess is somehow part of that provision. In a way, the rescuer goes along with the Messie's approach to provision.

However, it is all an illusion similar to the wizard in *The Wizard of Oz*. The Messie is not only *not* taking care of himself and the others in the house, he is actually harming the quality of life of those around him. On some level, both the Messie and the rescuer know that this is true. Neither will admit it, however, because the admission would shatter the illusion that the Messie, poor thing, is a strong and capable person. Even if the Messie wants it, this condescending and patronizing attitude toward the Messie is disrespectful and demeaning.

In this atmosphere where the Messie is put in charge but is incompetent, the MessieMate is often called upon to do the lion's share of the work but from behind the scenes. Sometimes the MessieMate asks and is given permission to do the necessary housekeeping jobs. As the MessieMate does the job, the Messie is supervising and griping that it is not being done just right. Sometimes the Messie forbids the MessieMate from doing something that is crying out to be done. All of this is consistent with the Messie's illusion of power. Even when the MessieMate is doing the job, the Messie has the say of how it is being done.

Asking permission to make basic housekeeping improvements is an attempt to confirm the Messie's leadership. Some MessieMates follow their Messie's directions no matter how unfruitful they may be. Trying to meet the Messie's need for self-esteem by pretending he is capable in an area in which he is not is really doing him a disservice. This pretending also allows the destructive behavior to continue. More important for the focus of this book, if you are participating in this pretense to any degree, you are doing yourself a disservice as well.

Please understand that I am not advocating a wholesale rebellion or rupture in the relationship. Take things slowly. Be wise in how you evaluate what is happening and what you want to do about your situation. The person who lives with a Messie will do well to leave games behind and go about living in a realistic and responsible way that will be good for all concerned.

If You Don't Plan to Change, Don't Complain about the Situation

Let's say that to keep your relationship on an even keel, you decide to let things go on as they are. You minimize your desires even while deep within you rages a hunger for beauty and order. You feel too miserable with the status quo to stay where you are, and you feel too frightened of change to move ahead.

At this point it's easy to start complaining. Like arguing and nagging, complaining gives the illusion of going

> *If you make a few changes*
> *but then stop, be thankful*
> *for the progress you've made.*

ahead, of making change, but it does not require any action on your part to leave the safety of your old ways. Complaining is the perfect cover for continuing dependency for the person who chooses to be a victim but doesn't want to admit it. You are willing to weep, to hate the house, to do anything but leave the warmth and safety of the status quo.

Avoid complaining so that you can more clearly see your situation: There ain't no fairy godmother, and you ain't no Cinderella. There is a principle in life: You reap what you sow. Your house is the way it is now as a result of a myriad of small decisions you have made in the past. The house will change in the future when you begin to make different decisions. It won't happen overnight. Patience is a priority. It will take time for any sown crop to be reaped. But be assured that just as surely as you take a step in any direction today, the decision will be acted out in your life in some tomorrow.

Stop the cover-up of complaining. Be willing to see what you really want and to see that you are not taking responsibility for what to do about those wants.

You may decide to make changes. Perhaps you will not. Perhaps you will decide to put off deciding. Respect yourself for any decision made *thoughtfully*. If you make a few changes but then stop, be thankful for the progress you've made. Acknowledge that you've made choices and don't complain about where you are.

Do Maintain a Healthy Neutrality

Now for one *do* for those of you who decide to step ahead with change. As you get a goal in sight, you may be tempted to focus even more on the Messie, the mess, and getting both straightened out. But a detachment is necessary. You can learn to care about the mess without taking on the job of clearing it up. You can express your concern that the Messie is having such a hard time with his clutter, if that is the case, but let him know that your life will go on well whether it gets cleared up or not.

When a "fixer" first begins to pull away from the life of fixing, the tendency is to go too far the other way and to isolate from the Messie. "You go your way; I'll go mine" is not a healthy neutrality. Healthy neutrality means you have detached yourself from the Messie's success or failure. Letting the Messie be responsible for his own life is a gift you give—the gift of freedom from your trying to fix and control.

It may not be possible to understand how to do this or to do it alone even when you think you understand how it should work. Group support is important when you try to make these changes. In a later chapter I'll say more about how to find support (see chapter 12).

Perhaps you will feel arrogant and self-centered when you begin to move away from enmeshment with the Messie's problem. The Messie may also feel this about you and tell you so. As long as you maintain in your heart and actions your concern for the Messie's highest good, you need not be concerned about your negative feelings about detachment.

When you make changes to a new way of life, you won't always do it right. You're learning something new. You are a novice. Sometimes you will slip into an inappropriate attitude. You are, after all, not perfect. Don't let that derail you from your goal. Things will begin to right themselves as you go along. You will learn. You will not continue to confuse independence with autonomy or detachment with arrogance or caring with pitying. If things go right, you will experience both a responsible independence within yourself and an intimacy with the Messie that would be impossible as long as you continue to try to rescue him.

I think that this condition is called a healthy relationship. Or maybe it is just called *love*.

Chapter 7

Setting Your Goal and Stepping Out

Rebecca married Ken seven years ago. She has an eleven-year-old son from a previous marriage. Before she married Ken she knew he was disorganized, but she thought she could change him. Reasonably organized herself, she underestimated the extent of the problem. Seven years later, Ken has not changed. The house is "a nightmare," she says. Ken won't let her get rid of anything. "Everything has sentiment. Everything has great potential value."

Sometimes when Ken is away on business, she thins out his clothes or papers a little, but only in such a way that he is not really aware that anything is gone. Once she got rid of an old rocking chair that she had been advised was worth little. Ken was furious. To him, it was a valuable antique. Gone! Rebecca learned not to over-step her moderate, secretive system of thinning things out a little at a time. "I hate to sneak around like that," she admits, "but what else can I do?"

That minimal kind of discarding in the face of all Ken brings in and keeps makes Rebecca's effort hardly worth-while. She has tried being strict. She has tried being kind.

> *The light of wisdom does not shine very far down the path. Things will become clearer as you take one step at a time.*

She has appealed to Ken to change for his and for her sake. But nothing has worked. She can't have friends over at all, and her son never brings friends home. Rebecca has read the book *Messie No More*. She tried to get Ken to look at it, but he is not interested. The book helped her to understand him better, but it has done nothing to change him. In the meantime, as a practical measure, Rebecca has taken over the finances.

Ken is a wonderful man in many ways. Rebecca went into this thing with her eyes open even if her optimism about the possibility of changing Ken was misplaced. Perhaps his disorganized ways were a challenge to her. She could help and love him into a better way of life. But Ken's clutter has continued unabated. A well-balanced and outgoing woman, Rebecca is able to live with this burden with the same good humor, intelligence, and courage that she would bring to any problem in her life.

Perhaps you relate to Rebecca's story in some way. You,

like her, wonder what to do next. We're at the point where the rubber meets the road of your plans for the future. Where do you go from here?

Now is the time to put aside guesses about what makes the Messie tick, hopes that he will change, and anything else that may distract you from the real issue: How are you going to make your own life satisfactory, even charming and enjoyable, at this point even if the Messie does not change in character?

I hope you have decided to give your Messie his freedom—freedom to change or not as he sees fit. Actually, you do not give, or take, the freedom of anyone. You only recognize and live in the light of the fact that you cannot force anyone to change. You entrust him or her to the care of God, who does have the power to change people. You would sincerely like for the Messie to change. You certainly hope he or she does. But you have given up demanding that it be so. That is not your area of responsibility. Your responsibility is for your own life.

So you turn your attention to yourself. You are ready to change. Let us concentrate on the practicality of the house, not because we are going to become house focused, but because the house is part of your focus on your own needs. As you handle the house problems, you will begin to bring about the changes within yourself that you seek.

Choosing a Specific Goal

You feel your attitude is right, and you're ready for action? Start thinking in terms of a specific thing you want changed about the house. Choose a specific short-term goal. It is best not to map out a whole panorama of change. The light of wisdom does not shine very far down the path. Things will become clearer as you take one step at a time.

Just choose one thing about the house (notice I did not say to choose one thing about the Messie) that you want to be different or to work differently. It should be something that is bothersome to you at this present time.

Here are some suggestions to get you thinking:

- I will not have a messy living room.
- I will not allow the table by the door to be used as a dumping ground.
- I will not have a cluttered dining room table.
- I will not allow toys in the living room. Or I will not allow toys to be left in the living room when children are finished playing with them. Or I will allow only two toys at a time in the living room.
- I will not allow the beds to be unmade all day.

Choose just one. Start at whatever point you choose and move slowly into other areas as you see how it works for you.

Setting this kind of goal is hard for many people. It seems so selfish. I hope you are beginning to see the reasonableness of this kind of self-orientation.

Several problems arise when people who are used to being helpers try to set and work toward goals. In the first place, they are not used to being proactive. They are basically reactive people. Setting goals breaks the reactive pattern. Second, these people usually live in the here and now. They like to be flexible and move with the activities as they present themselves. They say they are spontaneous. Setting goals is future-oriented and requires a certain steadfast dedication to something even in the face of fluctuating activities in the present. To set goals one must decide what one wants and act rather than react. It takes courage to commit to the future rather than to make spur-of-the-moment decisions.

Start Small

You do not need to change everything at once. As a matter of fact, the famous eighty-twenty rule applies here. How does it work? In business, for example, 20 percent of the sales reps close 80 percent of the sales. Or 20 percent of the customers purchase 80 percent of the merchandise sold. In high school, 20 percent of the students require 80 percent of the discipline. In our situation, this rule suggests that when you make a well-chosen 20 percent change, there will be an 80 percent result. This means that to have a significant change in your house, you need to target the few but important aspects that will make the difference.

> *Have an alternative plan*
> *in case things don't go well.*

Start slowly. Draw the line at different places and see how it fits your needs. One week you may have one bottom line. The next week you may find that you reevaluate it and are willing to settle for things to be either more or less messy in this place or that. Do not set your goals too low. Aim high. Make your goals specific. Name time and place. Keep beauty and dignity in mind. A beautiful house is the stuff of dreams. Anything less than a dream will not inspire you.

We tend to hit somewhere near where we aim. If we have a desirable goal, we will work for it. Get excited about your goal. Working for something you don't really want is disheartening, and you will quit when the going gets rough. So don't go for something you see as attainable but that will not meet your needs and make a difference in your quality of life. You must determine what your real ideals and values are.

In addition, be sure your bottom line is reasonable. You will not stick with a goal that you feel deep down is not fair to the other person. When you think about it, you can see that one of the hardest parts of this change is in clarifying just what it is you are aiming for.

At this point, why not stop and write down your bottom line on a three-by-five card? If you cannot get it down, you probably have not yet defined your goal. You know what you want, sort of. But only when you really know where you're heading do you have a chance to get there—and know you've made it.

Your Alternative Plan

Before you begin implementing any plan, establish an alternative plan in case your minimum requirement is not met. If the Messie will not allow you to achieve any change in the house, what will you do? You still have options. Will you begin to engage in life away from the house—taking classes or meeting friends in restaurants? Will you find a spot in the house and carve out an island of beauty and order where you can retreat and hibernate away from the winter of the disorder? Will you take up gardening and other outside pursuits? Will you have a cleaning woman in and invite friends over even though things are a wreck? If the Messie is an adult child or a roommate, will you ask him or her to move out?

There is no guarantee the Messie will allow you to make the bottom-line changes you feel are essential. That is, he may threaten the relationship over this issue in a way that makes you more uncomfortable than you are willing to tolerate. Or, though he may try to change, he may continue to maintain the messiness at a level higher than you can handle. He may stonewall and refuse to consider change. What will you do then? It is important that you settle this before you begin. I'll call this decision your best alternative.

Having a best alternative chosen will help you keep your head when things do not go right. You know clearly your goals and objectives. You have a plan in case things don't go well.

Accomplishing Your Goal

Your next step is to decide how you are going to accomplish your goal. There may be several parts to this step, and it may take some time to carry it out. Start by determining how you can make clear to your Messies your bottom-line *I-will-not* statement.

It might go like this: "Bill, kids, I want to keep this table by the front door clear. When you come in, take your books and tools on back where they belong." Then you get out the furniture polish, polish the piece nice and bright, and put a potted plant or glass figure on it. So far, so good. No one will object to this. It is reasonable and, after all, it is only talk. Perhaps the family will immediately start putting things where they belong. If so, you have accomplished your goal. Now choose another *I-will-not* statement and go from there.

However, it is unlikely that things will go this smoothly. Old habits die hard. Nobody likes to change. The family senses that you are just talking about keeping the table clear.

So let's suppose that the next day someone comes home, squeezes school books on a corner of the table, and goes into the kitchen for a snack. Expecting this, you have planned your next move.

"Karen, I want to keep that table clean and clear. Will you take your books to your room?" you state calmly.

"Just a minute! I'll get to it!" she calls, cookie in mouth.

You may choose to reply, "I don't want to wait a minute. Please move them now."

If she moves the books, great. If not, you now have another choice. You can have a big confrontation about obedience and responsibility. My suggestion, however, is that you speak with your actions. Wait a minute or so, whatever you are comfortable with, and take the books to Karen's room yourself. Don't say a word about it. I know it is not fair for you to do the work, but remember that your goal is to have a nice-looking table.

Perhaps Karen will say, "Mom, I told you I would do that!" Or, "Mom, why did you do that? I would have gotten them in a minute."

Your reply could be, "I want the table clear of books all the time." No fuss, no blame, just facts. Keep your goal in mind.

The next time Karen leaves her books on that table (you do think there will be a next time, don't you?), you put them somewhere else, maybe under her bed or in the basement. When she complains that she can't find them, tell her where they are. When she objects to where they are, suggest that when she puts them in her room, they are where she wants them. You keep escalating without recrimination or blame. Never fuss or be annoyed. You are out to keep the table clear, and that is what is happening.

If in frustration she says, "Mom, you are getting really kookie about that table!" do not defend yourself or explain what you are doing. Agree with her and say without rancor, "Yes, indeed I am. Remember that when you think about putting the books on the table."

Let us look at another example: a husband's clothes on the floor. If you have said you want to keep the floor clear and he continues to drop his clothes anywhere, put them in the hamper without saying a word. The next time and all subsequent times, put them in the back of the closet or under the bed or somewhere out of the way, so they are not cluttering the floor. Don't wash them. When he complains about having no clean underwear, explain that you did all the laundry in the hamper. His underwear was not in the hamper. If he would like to put his underwear there at any time, you will be happy to wash it with the rest of the laundry.

To Move the Messie's Stuff or Not?

This is a big question. In America, where freedom of choice and privacy is considered sacrosanct, many people would never consider touching someone else's things. Many people who live with Messies feel that it is wrong to violate another's personal space. If this is true, it always amazes me that the Messie so often gets away with violating the personal space of others by cluttering it. Even if Messies clutter only one side of the room, the beauty and tranquility of the whole room is violated when any part of it is out of place. Yet the people who live with Messies often feel that the Messie's personal space is off limits. If you feel strongly that way, you do not have the option of moving things out of your way because of your beliefs. You have limited yourself. That is all right. It just means that you have one less option in your life.

For now, consider my arguments: While it is important to act with respect and high regard for the Messie, it is also important to act in your own self-interest where there is an issue that you, in your own good judgment, have decided is worth the risk inherent in change. Respect for the Messie and your own self-interest are not mutually exclusive. If your Messie throws clothes on the floor of your common dressing room and insists that he

> *Moving the things that interfere with your minimal goals will make a strong statement about the seriousness of your intentions.*

does not want you to touch them because he wishes them to remain on the floor—in your way—until he gets around to picking them up, do not buy into this plan. Do not hit the ceiling. Be moderate. State dispassionately your case focusing on your own position concerning clothes on the floor. Give a little time for him to pick them up—however much time you are comfortable with. Then move the dirty clothes to wherever you plan—the laundry hamper, the back of the closet, under the bed, or wherever. If however, the Messie has his own dressing area, and the clothes on the floor do not involve you directly, leave the clothes there and close the door. Let the clothes pile to the ceiling if that is the desire of the Messie. It is not your concern, because it does not affect the graciousness of your life.

Remember, again, that your goal is not to change the Messie. It is all right to *want* to change him. That would certainly be desirable. But it just won't work. You can't change anyone else. You are just spinning your wheels and wasting energy to try it. Conserve your energy and use it to change your own actions and reactions. Let it go at that.

There will be many gray areas in trying to decide when to act toward moving someone else's things and when to let the mess remain. You do have the option of moving the Messie's things if you have laid the groundwork of deciding where you will draw a line and if you've communicated that message to the Messie in a few non-blaming words. Moving the things that interfere with your minimal goals will make a strong statement about the seriousness of your intentions.

Some readers will object that they should not have to pick up the Messie's clothes. They feel that each person should pick up his or her own clothes. I agree, but *shoulds* aren't the issue here. As long as you allow *shoulds* to hem

> *The Messie loves his things,*
> *but he hates the hold the belongings have on him.*

in your options, you are giving away your power over your own life. Once you break out of this rigid viewpoint and allow yourself more flexibility of action, you empower yourself. Consider it. Perhaps you might try it. You might find you have discovered an important and powerful tool.

To Throw Away the Messie's Stuff or Not?

This is an even bigger question than whether to move the Messie's stuff out of your way. I can tell you from the perspective of a bona fide Messie—Messies take their belongings very seriously.

Before we go any further with this hot topic, let me remind you of one of the tenets of this book. We do not consider dealing with the Messie's things for the benefit of the Messie—to do him a favor. We focus on ourselves.

If the junk the Messie has is significantly interfering with our lives, we consider the possibility of removing it from where it is doing that interfering to some place where it will not interfere.

This is not an easy thing to do because Messies have a feeling—not a thought, mind you, a feeling—that the cherished belongings are somehow alive like pets and that the Messie is morally responsible for their well-being. That is why Messies want to give them away to a good home where they will be properly valued and cared for. As with an old and faithful dog, the Messie does not casually evict his junk.

Messies also have the feeling—again, not a clear thought, but a vague feeling—that some part of the former owner is mixed with the belongings. If the old plate belonged to Aunt Nan who is deceased, a little of Aunt Nan somehow lives on in that plate. When the plate is gone, she will be gone altogether. Often the Messie feels that some part of himself is wrapped up in the belonging. If it is discarded, some part of himself is lost. He is diminished. We are not talking reason here; we are talking emotions so deep the Messie is only vaguely aware of them. At every turn he bumps into the invisible wall of discomfort when he tries to get rid of something.

Messies live with fear of being without what they need. If they have a lot of stuff, they feel safe, cared for. To get rid of anything is to risk kicking up that old fear of being in need.

The Messie loves his things, but he hates the hold the belongings have on him. In some cases, it is a blessing for someone to come into the picture and move things along. In my case, the order and beauty my mother provided for me as a child—by handling the comings and goings of my things—was a real gift to me. Because I had all of the characteristics of a Messie even as a child, it would have been a burden for me to have had to make decisions about getting rid of things that obviously had to go.

However, children grow up and Mommy isn't there to take care of those hard decisions anymore. The buck stops with each adult to do his own tossing out. That is where the Messie begins to get in trouble. He drags his feet; he procrastinates; he hangs onto things. And *you* have to live with the results of his fears.

Should you get rid of the stuff for the Messie and save him the distress of having to do it? It would be a little like taking that old, faithful but ailing pet dog down to the vet for his final visit. The person who does that hard job is frequently sparing the feelings of all the others who loved that fine animal and cannot bear to see him go. That is the way it is in most cases. (In other cases, of course, those who love him want to be with him until the final moment.)

I am suggesting that sometimes you do yourself and the Messie a favor to take over and move stuff out if you have his knowledge and permission. At other times, where the Messie strongly objects, you cannot get rid of the beloved possessions without hurting him and your relationship. Again, I recommend that you not consider dealing with any belongings except those that directly interfere with your life. If the belongings do not directly interfere with you either because they make the house hard to use or because they make it ugly, do not even consider moving them or getting rid of them.

Now comes the question of how to do the deed. First, you tell the Messie that you are going to be working to clean up the room, organize the closet, reorganize the garage, or whatever. He will probably warn you to leave his things alone. Tell him that you won't do anything with his things without talking to him about it. Wait a few days before you do anything. Fast movement makes Messies nervous. They need time to adjust to the idea that anything will be touched.

Put the junk that you think needs to be thrown out into a box. Label the box with a sign such as "old, outgrown clothes" and include a discard date two weeks or so in the future. Tell the Messie that you have put some of the clothes he doesn't or can't wear anymore in a box in the garage; it is there so that if he wants anything, he can get it. Explain the cutoff date: Whatever is still there then will go to Goodwill or the Salvation Army. Now the ball is in his court. He may or may not dip into the box. That is up to him.

Do all of this in a very detached way. State your plans clearly but simply. Speak in an offhand way. Don't rush into it. If possible, do the sorting and moving while the Messie is not home. Inform him immediately of what you have done.

Some Messies will be very upset; others will be mildly annoyed. Recall the law of love. You do not wish to hurt him. You wish his highest good. But you have a legitimate need to live in a somewhat orderly environment. There has got to be compromising on both sides, not just yours. Talk about your needs. Ask him for his alternative. Be cooperative. But keep your goal in mind.

In some cases the junk is so outrageous that other approaches are necessary. Let us assume that the garage is jam-packed from floor to ceiling, from back to front. Nobody can get anything from it. You have not been able to get to the washer for years. The car sits in the driveway. You announce in the winter that, come spring, you want the garage cleared. You ask the Messie what he intends to do about it. If he doesn't know or it doesn't look as though he is moving toward a solution, you begin looking for a junk hauler. Line up a neighbor boy or someone to come over several weeks before the first load is to be hauled off. Tell your Messie of each step, again, in as casual a way as you can. The Messie knows deep down

By opening yourself to creative options, you will discover interesting approaches you could never have dreamed of before.

how serious the problem of the garage is. He just doesn't want to face it. He will object, but he knows in his heart of hearts that you are right to want the situation changed.

He might object that this is not a garage full of junk. It is a museum of valuable, irreplaceable collector's pieces. He forbids you to touch a thing. He will take care of it, he vows, just as soon as he gets around to it. Yes, indeed, very soon.

In this case, you cancel the junk hauler truck and tell the neighbor boy that you have changed your plans and won't need him. Then you state a date for when the junk will be removed. Negotiate that date with the Messie or just set it at a reasonably distant date. He has until that time to get around to it.

Have you failed because he refused to cooperate? Not at all. By your stating your position, making plans, calling the junk hauler and neighbor, you have stated your case and modeled how to go about it.

Suppose the negotiated date comes and goes and nothing is done. Now you need to reevaluate your course of action. Your options have been strengthened by all of this posturing. You have probably begun to see that further options are open to you. I hope you have begun to free yourself from the helplessness you once felt toward your situation with regard to the clutter. You are not a victim.

By opening yourself to creative options, you will discover interesting approaches you could never have dreamed of before. This variety of creative choices will begin to enhance the quality of your life.

Considering the Concerns of the Messie

You might think of options that meet underlying needs of the Messie. It may not be apparent that he has an agenda, but he does. You need to address his agenda if you wish to negotiate change. What will he settle for? What are his requirements? You will not be truly successful unless his needs as well as yours are met.

For instance, you may think that he wants to save piles of memorabilia when he may just want to preserve the memories those items represent. In that case, he might settle for taking a photo of the items and getting rid of the actual thing. A photo album with notations about dates and places might free the Messie to clean up a whole room of junk. This satisfactory alternative may never have occurred to the Messie.

Or a Messie may be saving piles of books he imagines to be of great value. A trip to the used book store may shock him into seeing that people won't take the books free, much less pay for them. I speak here as a Messie who went through this enlightening and humbling experience. It certainly freed me to get rid of books that I, in my naivete, had envisioned were treasures. Or the Messie may actually cash in on some of the books. You might suggest that life is short. Why wait until the books escalate to some unknown maximum value? In actuality the value of the books is usually not enough to pay the rent for the space they are occupying in your house. The point is, the Messie may not want the books as much as he wants the value. If you help him achieve the value or see that there is none, you won't be bothered with the books.

If you are aware of what the Messie really wants, you may be able to meet your needs and his at the same time. This is not supposed to be a win-lose contest between the two of you. I hope you will be able to make an arrangement in which both of you win. Deep down the Messie might be delighted to get rid of the clutter if his values are not sacrificed. There is a chance that he will agree to your proposals for change if his basic concerns are genuinely addressed. Your needs will most likely be met if you take the attitude that your desire is to solve the problem along with him. You two are partners in trying to live happily together.

Of course the fact has to be faced that perhaps the Messie will not want the pictures of the mementos. He may want the real thing and resent your suggesting otherwise. And he may not want the money for the books. He may want to keep the actual books till their imagined optimum value is reached. Or he may just really like to have the books at hand. In this case, perhaps you can negotiate getting a shed or renting a warehouse to keep the stuff. In some cases, such as the case of the man with the seven rental warehouse storage areas, storage is just an extension of the problem.

What I Will Not Do

In my own case, I have found that with patient caring on my part, staying way out of the part of the problem that belongs to the Messie, and sticking to my goals goes a long way toward keeping the house problem under control. I have my areas of concern. I want certain organizational basics to be met. These are areas for which I have responsibility. The Messie's problem in his own living area is not basically mine. Or if he had decided to solve his problem, I am not going to swing into action and help. Whether the Messie uses pictures to keep his treasures fresh in his memory or not, gets money for his books or not, gets a rental warehouse unit or not, is really none of my concern. I bring up these options in an attempt to negotiate to meet my own needs. I am certainly not going to buy the film to take the pictures as a hint. I am not going to look up the address of the used book store just to get him started in the right direction. I am not going to check on the prices of the rent of the warehouse unit for him. All of that stuff is his responsibility if it is in his private area. To get involved smacks of manipulation. The closer I stick to my own responsibility and leave his alone, the more likely it is that change will happen. If the Messie does nothing to take care of his responsibilities in a reasonable time, then I consider my options and may move things into a warehouse or some such solution.

I care about the Messie. I offer opportunities for change and for living with me in a way that meets my needs as well as his. He is not my enemy. I will attempt not to escalate the problem by taking a tough stand when patient understanding coupled with responsible talk and actions on my part will accomplish my goals and work for the benefit of the Messie. I will not try to cut through a knot that can be untied with patience. In the end, however, the choice of what he does with his private stuff in his private area is his.

Summary

Your task is clear:

- Resolve to improve the degrading living conditions that have been forced upon you.

- Let the Messie know your plans to throw something out long ahead of time.
- Speak reasonably and calmly.
- Don't go into detail.
- Give him a chance to retrieve his things.
- Do the deed when the Messie is not at home if possible.
- Speak with love and care.

If you do all of these things, the best-case scenario is that the Messie will be relieved and grateful that a job that had weighed heavily on him was done. More important from your perspective, your life will be better.

Of course, in the case of those with severe problems such as obsessive-compulsive disorders, this approach will probably not work at all. The best approach with more serious cases is through the techniques of a behavioral psychologist. If a Messie resorts to physical violence, it is important that you remove yourself from danger and seek professional help.

Listen to your own judgment. Then make your plans. Maintain flexibility in how you accomplish your goal, but be inflexible in your resolve that you will not continue to live as a victim of disorder.

With careful maneuvering and respect for the Messie, you'll make progress toward your goals. It will not be easy on anybody, but living with the mess is not easy either—for anyone. *Ease* is not part of the Messie picture. If the Messie looks clearly at the mental profit-and-loss statement of the situation, he will decide to abandon the cluttered lifestyle.

Chapter 8

Beyond Resistance

Perhaps this is a good place to stop and discuss what will likely happen to you and your Messies as you begin to implement changes. When you quit shielding them from responsibility and fussing at them, they will get the picture that you have changed. Change is uncomfortable for everyone. Somewhere along this route, you can expect the Messie to grow irritated and angry and try to get you to change back to your old pattern. He will test your resolve again and again. You'll be surprised at his potentially effective, ingenious ploys and words that push all the wrong buttons for you:

- You're really going overboard with this.
- What's wrong with you? Have you become a women's libber?
- What is this? PMS? (Or menopause?)
- You've become the most selfish person I've ever seen.
- Don't you care about your family anymore?
- Stop trying to run (or ruin) my life.

Ignore Bad-Mouthing

All of this bad-mouthing is a sign of recovery. Your changes are making a difference. Don't respond in anger. Go slowly. State your case with calmness, dignity, and love, and keep walking (not steamrolling) on the path before you.

Know that the Messie might actually succeed in stopping you if you have not:

- made a commitment to fulfill your own responsibility to yourself
- kept your goal firmly in sight
- relentlessly and wisely followed the path of giving the Messie the freedom to live his own life
- gone slowly and evaluated the effect of each step

If you have a healthy detachment, you can keep your cool and your resolve. Try to remember that this is not a win-lose contest. If all goes well, everybody will win.

Answer the recriminations with calm dignity and good humor in keeping with your personality. "Right, I joined the women's lib movement. I'm expecting my membership card any day now." Or, "Yes, this is PMS. That stands for Perpetually Moving Stuff—your stuff." A little humor never hurts.

Whatever you do, never justify your actions with accusations. "Well, I have told you again and again not to put your books there! You just won't listen. Now it has come to this. You made me do it this way. If I have told you children once, I've told you a thousand times, do not leave your books on that table. But do you listen? No. You don't hear a word I'm saying."

No, no, no. None of that. This is not a personal contest. You are just doing what is best for you. What you are doing is not unreasonable or wild. You are just insisting

> *Try to remember that this is not a win-lose contest. If all goes well, everybody will win.*

on reasonable and rational living for yourself. In whatever way you decide to implement the steps to your goal, calmness and dignity born of respect for yourself and your Messie will be your strength to carry them out. Don't talk with your mouth; talk with your behavior.

Special Issues of Resistance

The Messie Elderly Parent

The elderly parent or relative who is a Messie presents some special issues that might help an adult child better understand resistance to change. The older Messie might be using the excess of belongings to reassure herself that she will have what she needs as she grows less able to care for herself. She may also be feeling contradictory stress, sensing that as she grows more feeble, she will not be able to handle this great bulk of material and its disorder. She may fear the time when others will discover and have to deal with the extent of the disarray.

Older Messies often confide to me, "I don't want to die with things this way."

Yet when the younger family member starts making changes, the intrusion is often unwelcome because the older Messie so badly wants to maintain her independence. This overriding fear of dependence can exacerbate resistance to change.

In dealing with any older Messie, take special care to try and determine what benefits the Messie gets from the mess. I know of one older woman who got a lot of attention from church women who came in regularly to clean her house. She would have been a fool to clean up her act and give up the attention she was receiving. Surely the church women could have identified other ways to show their love and concern without enabling the clutter.

The Messie Child

Messie children fall into several categories that vary greatly in degree, cause, outcome, and onset of messiness. There is the Messie child who, like many other Messies, uses the clutter to take a stand for independence. Some children are not really Messies, but they try on messiness in the same way they might dye their hair red or get an earring. I call them pseudo-Messies. They just want to see what it would be like to live that way. Usually, they get tired of it and, if they possess the ability to do so, get back to a more organized way of life. In this case, if the children seem to be going through a phase, it is probably best to close the doors to their rooms until it blows over. If you do not help them find their books in the debris or help them clean up when their friends are coming over, it may blow over faster. Let them live with the consequences of their choices. This is, after all, not exactly a moral issue.

Then there is the early-onset Messie. I had it as a child. I was scatterbrained and would have been very disorganized if God had not given me a mother who created order in which I functioned in a reasonably organized fashion. Her contribution was a priceless gift to me as a child. For the most part, she did what needed to be done. I thought all houses were always orderly without effort. I was not aware of the seriousness of my weakness. I think that if she had tried to correct it in me as a child, she would not have gotten very far.

I feel an organized parent can often give the gift of order to a child who is too feeble in this area to do much for himself. When the child resists the help, because it is offered in an offensive way or because the child wants to exert independence, I suggest the loving but detached personal responsibility approach of this book. You've probably got a relationship problem not strictly related to clutter. The clutter may be the background against which a broader story is being played out. It can also be the stage on which many relational problems can be addressed and improved. If it accomplishes this good result, childhood messiness may be something of a blessing.

The Messie Husband

Messie husbands are usually messy for reasons that have nothing to do with their relationship to their wives. But a Messie husband may use his disorder as a power ploy. He does not want to be told what to do by his wife—it reminds him of his mother's treatment of him as a child. To keep his manhood, he resists change. Sometimes he may make the house incredibly messy and engage in outrageous behavior just to show the depth of his power. In short, he may use the house as a weapon in a struggle with his wife.

The Messie Wife

Interestingly enough, the Messie wife may also use the house as a weapon. If she feels powerless in the relationship or resentful or ignored, she may use the house in an attempt to solve some of her problems. If she perceives her husband as bossy, she can stonewall by not cleaning up. No matter how hard he pushes, he can't make her change in that area. Or she may just want his attention; when he is fussing at her about the condition of the house, she has it.

Please understand that she may actually find it almost impossible to get the house in order, and that fact may be a distress to her. That is the negative side. The positive side to her is that since the house is messy, she can at least use it to some advantage to dramatize her feelings.

Adriana's Response to Resistance

Let's look at an example of a MessieMate who encountered resistance. Consider how Adriana kept her goal in front of her but was also lovingly concerned for her husband.

Adriana is taking down the Christmas tree. The children are helping her put the decorations back into the boxes they've brought up from the basement. Adriana is in charge of what goes in what box and how. The next day when Adriana gets home from work, she takes the first of the packed boxes back to the basement. "Wait!" says Ralph, who was at work when the job was done. "Those boxes aren't ready to go yet!"

"Why not?"

"They aren't packed right. Some heavy things are on top of lighter stuff. It needs to be checked and rearranged.

One year we ruined a bunch of stuff by not putting it in the boxes right."

"Well, you do it if you aren't satisfied. I think it is fine myself." Adriana stopped to double-check the contents of all the boxes to make sure that they were satisfactory. She continued, "I'll take them downstairs. When you are ready, you can go down there and rearrange them."

"No! Leave them right there. I don't want them downstairs until they are right. We'll forget about them if they are out of sight. Last year we put them up and never went back to rearrange them. Some of the things were squashed. Just leave them right there!"

Adriana explains that boxes in the middle of the living room are not part of her plan for gracious decor. Ralph is adamant that "Do it right or not at all" is his motto. He says that she must understand that they are talking about *his* house, *his* decorations, and *his* principles. These are near sacred Christmas decorations. They are sort of family heirlooms, for Pete's sake. He will not have them violated. The boxes will stay in the living room until properly arranged.

At this point Adriana gets a flash of insight. If it is really all his, why is she working so hard on it? Why does she care at all? Then she realizes that it is not just his. It is hers too. She says, "If you want to rearrange them, please have it done by tomorrow, because I don't want them here after tomorrow."

True to his manhood and to his commitment to do the right thing, Ralph states that he will do it when he is good and ready, when he has time to really do it right.

"Wonderful," she says. "I appreciate your cooperation. I'm sure you can get it done by tomorrow night, because that's the latest I want them in the living room."

Ralph gives some retort about his not going to be coerced. Adriana does not say anything more. She has stated her case and her resolve. Later, she is especially kind and gentle to Ralph, because after all she does love him and wants his best good. Being loving is a particularly important issue to make clear at this point, because he is feeling threatened and anxious. He can continue to be as messy as he wants any time he wants as far as she is concerned just as long as it does not violate what she has defined as an important personal issue with her, in this case, the order of the living room. This is not some kind of contest for control. She just wants what is reasonable—a living room, not a warehouse. She just wants an orderly home.

In this whole scenario Adriana is keeping her relationship with Ralph in mind. For her, as for most women, relationships are extremely important, the top priority. Ralph, however, like many men, is strongly competitive. It is not her desire to turn this into some kind of power struggle if she can help it. This will stir up Ralph's desire to win and threaten the peace of her marriage. She must be willing to risk some of that peace temporarily for her own personal well-being, but if she overdoes it, she will lose more in the area of relationship than she gains in personal well-being. That is why the program I suggest has a minimum of talking, which can degenerate into squabbling. I also suggest that you move slowly and evaluate your moves reflectively. Finally, I emphasize that you keep the focus on yourself. Do not try to change the Messie. Focus on improving your own lifestyle, doing for yourself, taking personal responsibility, not on straightening him out.

The next evening if the boxes are packed, Adriana asks Ralph to help her take them down. If they are not, she asks if she can help him pack them, because it is her desire to put them downstairs that evening. If he says he will do it himself but does not, she doesn't threaten or fuss. But at the earliest convenience, preferably when Ralph is not home, Adriana takes them down to the basement. If Ralph has a fit, she asks if he would like her to bring them up so he can rearrange them before he puts them down in the basement. Always cooperative, always kind, but always keeping her goal sharply in focus. It is not an act. Her concern is for the house, but it is not against him.

Ralph may keep pushing, insisting on his way. At some point they will reach some kind of compromise. Adriana may end up on the losing end for the most part. But she may have scored some significant points, learned some things about standing up for herself, and set a tone different from her old ways. To reach her goal, it is not necessary to win every battle. Falling short of a goal is not a failure—it is a detour, not a dead end. I would tell Adriana not to expend energy on being upset if it doesn't work out as easily as she had hoped. She should just go on to her next goal, pleasantly and with as much loving detachment as possible.

Finally, Ralph may grow more and more agitated and go on the offensive. Thankfully he is not violent. If he were, Adriana's first concern would be to remove herself for her own safety and to seek counsel as to what course to follow in the light of physical abuse. But Ralph is not violent. He exerts his resistance in other ways. He may criticize her in whatever ways he has learned work well with her. He may threaten never ever to take the decorations to the basement if she doesn't let up—even if she is not nagging. Not to worry. Adriana should not take it personally or press unwisely. This is the normal, natural way people react when threatened with change. Adriana needs to move with slow deliberation and care. She remembers that marriage is an important relationship. She doesn't want to clean the house while making a shambles of her marriage. Fortunately, that is not necessary.

As you, like Adriana, try to follow whatever course you chart for yourself, take it slowly. Relax. You already know to evaluate at each step the effect of your changes on what is going on in your relationship. Be wise. Do not overdo. Even though there may be rough times, in the end, dignity, poise, and self-respect should make both the house and the marriage relationship better.

If a wise and loving desire to upgrade your living conditions from disastrous to gracious begins to destroy your marriage, you probably have some other serious issues that need to be addressed—and not through the house-keeping route. To look at it another way, however, improving your relationship in regard to the house will probably benefit other facets of your relationship.

Relationships are complex, and the area of the house may just be the playing field on which the deeper issues of the relationship are played out. Working out issues in the area of clutter may have ramifications in the whole relationship. The house may be part of a larger issue—the issue of defining one's self as a person to be respected. There is also the possibility that the struggle you are experiencing has its roots in some unresolved issue with your family of origin. However, all of this guessing about unresolved issues does not mean that improving the order of the house has to be abandoned until its true source is uncovered. Much can be done to improve your life by just improving your household environment.

Finally, three days after Adriana has said she does not want to have the boxes in the living room one more day, they are gone. Being a perfectionist, it took Ralph a while longer than anticipated because he had to get new, sturdier boxes and buy more packing tape. (He had some tape, he thought, but somehow it was misplaced in the Christmas rush. Is this typical, or what?) Adriana did not ride him these three days, because she did not feel helpless. She was aware that she could move the boxes downstairs at any time. Knowing this made her feel less anxious about them. She was willing to wait and not move precipitously. Smart woman.

Ralph knew she could move them at any time, too. He had begun to suspect that she would challenge him on this if he waited too long. It seemed wise to him to move them downstairs himself as soon as he could get his act together without appearing to rush. Smart man.

Your Own Resistance

A chapter called "Beyond Resistance" wouldn't be complete if I didn't touch again on your own resistance to change—even after you've made the initial decision to set your course. Because change makes you uncomfortable, your Messie's charges and threats will find ready soil to grow in your heart. Left alone, like weeds, your doubts will steal the nutrients of wisdom and resolve and smother your recovery.

There is also the problem of the sense of aloneness you will feel as you take responsibility for your own life. There is a strange discomfort in developing a strong and separate self. The old patterns, though frustrating, were comfortable. Having your life enmeshed with someone else's gave you a false sense of intimacy. When you begin to demonstrate independence and personal power, you lose that old feeling of closeness that the rescuing, I'll-fix-you-up approach offered. To leave the old ways behind is to grow up, and growing up is hard to do.

Is there any hope you will succeed in this venture of change? Yes, there is. The thing that will keep you going even in the light of all the resistance is that it is very

> *When you begin to demonstrate*
> *independence and personal power,*
> *you lose that old feeling of closeness*
> *that the rescuing,*
> *I'll-fix-you-up approach offered.*

painful to continue to live the way you are. It is hard on you. It is hard on the Messie. (Don't let the Messie convince you otherwise.) It is hard on the relationship. It is hard on the house.

Once having glimpsed a view of your own pain, can you ever return to being as placid about your part in this affair as you were before? Once having whiffed the fresh air of freedom from this burden of clutter, can you ever close the windows again and live in the stale air of disorder? Once having opened your eyes to the crippling effect your protection of the Messie's destructive habits has had on him, can you ever comfortably return to behavior that you now suspect encouraged those habits?

Perhaps you can. Most of us cannot. Perhaps you already know too much ever to return to the old ways of not taking responsibility for your behaviors. To put it another way, perhaps you have already read too much to turn back comfortably. As always, the choice of whether to continue changing or not is yours.

Breaking Out of Isolation

To help you keep your resolve, reach out of yourself for friendship and support. Messiness is a lonely disease. People who will admit to almost any other problem are reluctant to talk about this one. I often say that Messies are the last group to come out of the closet, partly because we can't find our way out through all that stuff. But the real reason we are so reluctant to come out of the closet is that we are so ashamed about how we live.

This shame applies to the Messie's family as well. Children don't want to invite friends over; adults keep friends away, preferring to meet them elsewhere or dropping friendships altogether. Not having a house to share with friends curtails friendship development.

The Messie's family becomes more isolated and lonely. They become each other's only friends. This makes breaking out of the unhealthy parts of the relationship even harder. If some isolation has crept into your life, reach out. Friends and socializing are an important part of the richness of life.

When I woke up from the craziness of being a Messie, I saw how isolated I had become. I had many acquain-

> *If you've been adjusting your social life*
> *to the problem, stop.*

tances but only one friend—a friendship I did not maintain carefully. I thought, I suppose, that I was "perfectly all right with just me alone and my stuff to support me, thank you."

I was wrong. I did need social interaction. When I realized this, I was left with the job of starting new friendships—not an easy task for someone who had so little practice or skill. I wanted five friends, because I had read in a popular women's magazine that five was the average number of friends that happy women had. I have four friends now, and a fifth friendship is developing. One friend is moving away, so I will have to seek a replacement, if *replacement* can be used when talking about warm relationships. I will never quite replace my absent friend.

Now that I have these friendships, the house means so much more to me because it is a way I can share myself by expressing myself in my decor and style of entertaining. My house is a part of me that I can share. Since I live with a practicing Messie at this time, it is not always easy.

If you've been adjusting your social life to the problem, stop. Maybe it's time the problem adjusted itself to your social life. Getting out of the pattern of isolation will help you combat your own resistance and lack of courage.

Beware of Your Desire to Turn Your Back

When a fixer first begins to let go of taking care of the other person and starts to take care of herself, she often swings to the extreme of distancing herself from the source of her problem, the Messie. But either extreme—being too involved or being too distant—is focused on the Messie and is a reaction to his behavior. Both extremes are to be avoided. Of course old habits die hard, and stress heightens extremism. Sometimes we will slip into the old way of trying to force the Messie to change. Sometimes we will give up in disgust and become angry and impatient with the Messie and the situation.

When these things happen, it is important to try to get on a more reflective path—to return to the pattern of evaluating the situation calmly in its broader aspects. Talking to others who can listen in a detached way without trying to advise or "fix" you can be very helpful in enabling you to get your perspective back. You may be interested in starting a group for those who live with chronic Messies using this book as a basis for discussion.

The temptation to distance oneself serves a very useful purpose because it provides immediate relief from tension. We say to ourselves, and perhaps to them, that we do not care how they live. We emotionally divorce ourselves from feelings of compassion. We divorce ourselves from the Messie. In distress, we don't detach from the problem in a healthy way; we turn our backs on the whole thing. This kind of noncaring leads us away from intimacy with the Messie. Although "distancing" offers us temporary relief from stress, eventually it brings with it more anxiety than we had before we turned our backs.

Again, the attitude of the Messie toward the mess or toward us is not our responsibility. Our responsibility is our own attitude. Time after time we are called upon to seek the maturity to balance our lives. We neither get inappropriately involved in the Messie's life nor do we cut ourselves off from it. The God who saw us in our need and in our blindness to the chaos around us and yet stuck with us calls us to love the Messie—neither demanding that the Messie go our way nor ignoring the Messie altogether. Nothing less than true love will do. We love the Messies enough to accept them the way they are without accepting that we are stuck in a hopeless situation because of the way they are. Loving is hard—especially when we feel angry or frustrated. But it is our goal. It is our possibility.

Abandon Your Superior Role and Share Your Feelings

One of the best ways to avoid distancing from the Messie is to abandon the "I'm superior" role or act. Yes, you're eons ahead when it comes to housekeeping. You always remember birthdays early enough to get cards to the recipients on time. You throw things away without a qualm. But there is more to the story than this. You have your problems too. To act as though you don't only broadens the distance between the Messie and yourself.

Let us use as an example the scenario about the books on the entryway table. The mother kept a strong but light-hearted approach to the problem, and in her case that was probably appropriate. However, at some point, it would have been a good idea to share an I-statement that carried a more substantive message to the Messie. Some-where along the line, the mom could have stated her own

Mutual sharing will clear the air and disarm some of the tension building up because you are changing.

issues with household order: "When I was a kid, my mom always kept such a cluttered house that I was embarrassed to bring my friends home from school. I know that clutter doesn't bother you in the same way it did me; I guess we are different in that way. Anyway, even though I am an adult now, when I see things out of place, especially when they are where someone who is coming to visit will see them, I still feel like I did as a kid."

Notice that there is no appeal here for understanding or change on the part of the Messie. There is simply a low-keyed, straightforward statement of self-disclosure given in a nonjudgmental way. Since the mom is stating her own feelings, her thoughts, and her experiences, no one can legitimately argue with them. This kind of sharing validates her position. Letting the Messie know you also experience problems will help to diffuse the Messie's resentment and lower his anxiety. This type of statement signals that you are not distancing yourself from the Messie emotionally even though you have differing views about the condition of the house; it will open doors to intimacy. In the end, the goal is to get the house beautiful and orderly and to encourage a gracious and close relationship with the Messie.

Encourage Rational Conversation

Another way to diffuse building tension and misunderstanding is to engage the Messie in conversation by asking questions that relate to the subject of order in the home.

- Did your mom work outside the home as I do?
- Who did what chores when you were a kid?
- How did you feel about your mother's method for distributing the work?
- Did your family have household help come in to clean?
- Your mom and dad always have such an organized house and don't seem to work at it. It seems to come naturally to them. What do you suppose is their secret?
- If our house were organized and looked good most of the time, what do you think we would do differently? Would you like to have more company?

- Would it be nicer or worse for you if the house were pretty and orderly?
- What is it about having an organized house that makes you uncomfortable?

These questions should not be asked all at once, and you might share your own childhood experiences or feelings. When it seems appropriate, such mutual sharing will clear the air and disarm some of the tension building up because you are changing. The discussions may enable you to see new aspects of the problem. In most cases, they will signal a respect and appreciation for the feelings and thoughts of the Messie.

In some cases the topic of messiness is so sensitive and the relational tension so strong that even innocuous questions will stir up strife. In that case, you may choose to drop the subject with little or no comment. The fact that you even asked the question reinforces the change in you. If the Messie becomes upset and attacks you and your ideas, a nondefensive statement about your own interests is always in order. Something such as, "I see we really have different ideas about this" said with a smile will do. Make every effort to stay close to the Messie without rancor. If you distance yourself from the Messie at points like this, things tend to stay stuck and not progress.

The Forever Struggle

Will the rest of your life be a struggle to get one place cleaned up and then another? At first it looks like that because you are establishing your own boundaries and testing your own strength in achieving your goals. But you are not just getting the books off the entryway table. And you are not just getting the garage cleaned or the

Christmas decorations put in the basement or the clothes picked up off the dressing-room floor. Each of these incidents is a symbol of a whole new way of life for you, a life in which you take control of an important aspect of your own existence.

You used to be helpless; now you have options. You used to be rigid; now you are creative. You used to defer to everyone else's needs and desires; now you respect your own as well. You used to try to take care of others; now you offer them the freedom of their own choices. You used to expect someone else to rescue you from your unhappiness; now you know that your rescuer is you.

This change in you will begin to have a global application to the house. If all goes well, after a while, things will begin to upgrade without all this attention to the detail of each improvement. Your sights will be lifted; so will those of the Messies in your life. The house will reflect those changes.

Chapter 9

Maintaining Integrity and Negotiating Change

The Flood Disaster

Due to faulty grading, water drains into the basement of the new home of Myra and Phil, soaking boxes of books, papers, magazines, and general memorabilia that are important to Phil. Myra calls Phil at work and tells him of the problem. She suggests a solution: She could hire two teenage boys from the neighborhood to come and clear out the soggy mess. (It was a dry mess before the flood.) Phil will not hear of it. Those are valuable items.

They must be handled with care. Besides, it is a poor use of money to pay for what he can do. He will take care of it this weekend, he assures her. He does not tell her that one reason he is uncomfortable with her suggestion is because on some level he does not want any of the neighbors to know his secret, that he is a Messie.

> *You want to come alongside the Messie*
> *as a partner so that together*
> *you can meet the needs you both have.*

Myra is distressed. She knows that Phil is a procrastinator, and that he would rather do anything than tackle his junk pile. But she follows Phil's wishes and waits for the weekend. By the weekend the piles are smelling of mildew and are growing various kinds of fungus and mold. Phil has a really busy weekend. On top of that, he is very tired and cannot get to the boxes. But he will, he tells Myra.

Myra states that she does not want to live with the situation downstairs. She reminds him that she has to do laundry down there. She doesn't want to live with stench. "When you let things go, Phil," she says, "I feel nervous because I am afraid things are going to get too bad to ever be taken care of. I really want you to take care of it soon or to hire someone else to do it."

Phil responds with the words she has learned to fear: "I'll take care of it myself." He lies down to rest up, so he can get to it as soon as he has strength. Out of deference to Phil, we need to realize how hard the task is for him. It is like having to shoot that favorite family pet we mentioned earlier. The next weekend Phil is also busy.

On Monday Myra switches to her "best alternative" plan. She has the stinking mess carried out by the two boys. She pays them twenty dollars each. She divides the boxes into two groups. She puts the "totally ruined" out in the alley. A few that were on top and are sort of okay she puts in the garage. When Phil comes home he is livid. Underneath the anger is a certain sense of relief that the job is done, but he does not express that or even stop to recognize it himself.

Without rancor, Myra informs him that he may wish to check the ruined boxes out in the alley to see if anything is salvageable before the garbage men come on Wednesday. She also states that the not-so-ruined boxes are in the garage for his attention. In the meantime, she has scrubbed the basement floor with bleach. She tells him that the walls behind the boxes have a lot of mold now and need to be painted. She suggests that they have someone come in and do it. Phil says no, he will get to it next weekend. "Great!" Myra says. In the meantime, she begins to look around for a painter, just in case.

Actions and Words

If you have been reading carefully, you will realize that the Messie will not pay much attention to you until you change your actions. Messies who use their power to keep the house the way they like it will respect your power only if you prove it with action. You have probably talked until you are blue in the face in the past and nothing has changed. This chapter will give more insight about negotiating—talking—with a Messie. *What possible good will that do,* you ask, *since talking is so ineffective?*

Remember, again, that you are not trying to win over the Messie. You want to come alongside the Messie as a partner so that together you can meet the needs you both have. Toward this end, especially in some cases where the Messie is somewhat amenable to change, negotiating may be able to move the house along to a considerable extent in the right direction. Isaiah 30:15 includes a wisdom-filled line: "In quietness and in confidence shall be your strength" (KJV). The effective talk I'm advocating is not nagging or ranting; it is loving, quiet, and confident.

This kind of talk has a place. It does three things. First, it can be evidence of your strength for change, your difference in attitude. You are no longer willing to live in clutter. In a hundred little ways in what you say and how you say it, you will signal a powerful fact, that you have changed internally. Second, confident talking is, in a way, an action. Not a powerful one, but an action nonetheless. It has its place in your change of action. Third, it will explain what your actions are all about. Words and actions work together.

When to speak, when to draw a line, when to accept, when to impose consequences—these are all choices you must make wisely. My tendency is to err on the side of saying too much. I try to choose with care those times when I will speak. When I do say something, there is almost always agitated resistance. But things seem to move along well if I stick to I-messages and refrain from attacking the Messie with statements such as, "You are always ruining everything I get. You knew you had chocolate on your hands. Why didn't you wash them off?"

The Negotiating Power of I-Statements

It is unreasonable in the name of detachment to restrict mentioning some of the outrageous things the Messies do. No matter how polite and gentle one tries to be, if someone steps on your foot it is considered permissible to ask her to get off your foot. So it is in living with someone who steps on your organizational toes. If the Messie takes your hammer and doesn't put it back, it is perfectly permissible to say, "Put back my hammer whenever you use it."

If the Messie gets chocolate on your new book, it is perfectly all right to say, "When you get chocolate on my new book, I feel very sad, even angry, because I want to keep things nice. Either don't borrow my books or keep them clean."

Notice that there is no attack on the person. There is no "You are so clumsy," or "You are such a pig." What this statement does contain is a clear statement of how you feel. The focus is on your feelings. This cuts down on arguing, because who can deny how you feel? (By the way, don't overuse "I feel angry," or you will end up sounding as if you are attacking the person even though you are not.)

There are several steps to an effective I-statement. The first part is the *when* of the statement. "*When* you get chocolate on my book . . ." The next part is "I feel . . ." The third part is "because . . ." Finally, you state your alternative—what you want.

Here are more examples of I-statements:

- *When* you take my clothes to wear without asking, *I feel* frustrated *because* I don't have what I need to wear and I don't even know where my clothes are. Always *ask* when you want to borrow something.
- *When* you wax the car and leave the wax outside, *I feel* as if things are out of control *because* I need to have things where they are not lost or ruined. Please *put* the car wax back when you use it.

Of course, if you speak to the Messie about every disorganized thing he does, you would have a continuous one-way conversation all day long. Choose only one item to mention every once in a while when it really impacts your life in a personal way.

Making Daily Choices

Recently my Messie lost his key to the back door. He borrowed mine to get another key made. Being a procrastinator, he kept my key for several days without making another one. This meant that I could not go in and out the back door when I was home alone. Finally, I asked for my key back. *I* would have the extra key made, I said. That way the person who lost the key—not I—would be inconvenienced by not having a key. The Messie resisted this solution and vowed to get it made the next day. I gave him the grace of a day, and he had the copy made. If he had not, I would have insisted on having my key returned, and I would have had another made at my own convenience.

Another day my Messie spilled something on the microwave turntable. In his perfectionism he decided to give it a whiz-bang cleanup. He sprayed it with liquid cleaner but then walked away and left the turntable on the kitchen counter for three days. Each day he had good intentions of rinsing it off and putting it back in the microwave. Each night the unrinsed turntable sat on the counter. When I said something on the third day, he attacked, saying that I had been just as negligent in my own days of messiness. (This was true.) He continued that it was inconceivable that I should complain about him. I repeated my thought that the turntable belonged in the microwave, not unrinsed on the counter, that jobs started should be finished. He said huffily that it would be done by the end of the day.

In fact, by the next dawn the turntable was still unrinsed on the counter. I rinsed it and put it back in the microwave. It was a very simple task. I had left it out for three days—my limit of tolerance for that item. After all,

> *Misplaced principles can be
> a powerful deterrent to success.*

it *was* the job of the Messie to finish what was started. Leaving it out was my way of saying that each of us is responsible for his or her actions. In this case my enterprise was not successful if you look at the outcome. But it was in keeping with my integrity. It was one small step forward in a long journey. My washing it and putting it back did not make waves in our relationship. I did not allow it to frustrate me. I think perhaps it was a useful activity in keeping the line of my expectations drawn.

In my situation, these kinds of communications go a long way toward keeping things from getting totally out of control. In any situation that does not directly impact my life, I say nothing. Many situations that affect my life less directly I overlook or work around without comment or without consequences. On occasion, I tolerate not getting cooperation on something that is important to me for the sake of the relationship. But remember that one cannot avoid stating one's case on every issue without being deselfed.

My willingness to do unilaterally what I want done when necessary to achieve my goal—such as making the key or rinsing the turntable—is a powerful tool for me, because it allows me to accomplish my goal of having an orderly life without having to depend on the Messie. My willingness to do these things is owning my power, not abrogating it because I think I *should* not have to do someone else's job. Misplaced principles can be a powerful deterrent to success.

In some cases, such as the chocolate on the book, nothing can be done about the past incident. There is change to be made in future actions.

I am willing to wait for some things to change. Other things are negotiable. I cannot expect to solve all of my problems completely at once. If I had wished to have a totally problem-free life unbothered by anyone else, I could have chosen to live alone. Because I choose to live with others, there will always be some relational problems. Because I have chosen to live with a Messie (though not deliberately I can assure you) I can anticipate problems with disorganization. The real difficulty comes when I give up too much of myself to the relationship. It is up to me to make sure that does not happen by defining what areas are really important and sticking by those.

Negotiating When the Messie Asks for Your Help

What if your Messie truly seems to want your help in getting organized? If the Messie asks you for help in getting organized, you may wish to consider it. You may even wish to try it—once. Only you can make that decision. My best judgment is that in some cases where the Messie asks for help, he is attempting to avoid his own responsibilities and get you back into your position of being the family fixer. That kind of relationship only hinders progress for everyone.

But every situation is different. I have recently been

talking with a male Messie who lives with a Cleanie wife. He sincerely wants to clean up his act and please her, and he sincerely seems not to know how to go about it. He says that if his wife were to give him a detailed list of exactly what to do, he would gladly follow her instructions.

Actually, the Messie husband and Cleanie wife combination is one of the easiest to handle if the husband sees his wife's abilities as a benefit to him. After all, it is traditional for women to bring structure to men's lives—as secretaries, wives, or mothers. It can also work the other way, if a Messie wife cooperates with a Cleanie husband and sees his abilities as being to her advantage. Occasionally a neat husband will take over the total organization of the home and let his relieved wife use the system he has set up.

Do you offer help if asked for it? Again, you know what hasn't worked in the past. You know your goal, and you know your motives. (If you're seeking to control him, beware.) You're free to pursue various negotiating options as you see them.

If your Messie sincerely wants to change but seems to be suffering from an obsessive-compulsive disorder, a negotiating option might be that he agree to see a behavioral psychologist who has successfully treated OCD patients. Does that mean you drive him to the appointment? No, but neither do you hide the car keys on the day of his appointment.

One warning: Do not get so excited at initial signs of change that you help too much too early.

The Negotiating Dialogue

A negotiating technique for more difficult situations is suggested by Lehmkuhl and Lamping in their book *Orga-*

nizing for the Creative Person. As you know, when you
are in a conflict with someone else, it is important to
decide what you are willing to settle for, what your bottom line is, what you are willing to do, and what you are
not willing to do. This may not be obvious to you as you
begin to talk to your Messie about the problem. As you
use the negotiating dialogue technique, your desires may
crystallize more clearly. Here is an example.

Let's say your son Fred is a college student living at
home. He likes to study at the dining room table so he
can keep an eye on the nearby TV. When he becomes
tired, he gets up and walks away from the pile of books
and goes on to other pursuits. He plans to return (1) at
any moment, (2) when the urge hits him, or (3) when the
deadline is hard upon him. He wants his books left just
as they are so he will not lose any time regrouping when
he decides to return. His memory is poor for that kind of
thing, and he is afraid that if anything is changed, he will
forget where he is and what he is doing.

The first step is to state your request. You approach
him and say, "I want to use the table for eating. Will you
please move the books and things off the table so I can
set out the dishes?"

This is not satisfactory to Fred, who states his position.
"I don't want to move the books off the table, but I will shift
them down the table so you can get the three plates on."

If you reply that such a solution is not satisfactory to
you, you need to state what would be acceptable. "It is
not acceptable to me to have books piled on the table
while we eat. I wouldn't mind if we moved them all, just
as they are, to your desk in the back room and then move
the little black-and-white TV back there where you can
see it while you work."

Back and forth it goes until you arrive at a position you

can both live with. This is a reasonable and fair approach. It often works. At its heart is the desire to find a solution that meets the needs of both. As an adult-to-adult, non-defensive, and noncritical system, it makes a lot of sense.

However, as you know, people are not always rational. When you explain the system or make your request, Fred may say, "I'm tired of all this talking about minutia. You make too much of every little thing. You'd talk forever about everything if I let you. Just shift the books down the table and let it go at that!"

Now you have unilateral choices. You can always move the books yourself or use some other technique previously discussed.

When Things Don't Turn Around

Things aren't working. You want to attack. Don't. It will only drain off your energy and keep the situation stuck.

> *This problem may be one of the best things that ever happened to you, because it forces you into a self-examination you would not otherwise consider.*

Or you might want to give up. You are afraid that your relationship will be dashed. In your heart of hearts, you aren't really sure that you should be making these changes anyway. Try to summon the courage to stick with what you have determined is a reasonable and fair alternative. Don't give in too soon. Give your plan a chance.

A third possibility is that you might decide to just bail

out. If your Messie is a roommate or coworker you can easily move away from, this may be a good alternative. If, however, it is a commitment such as marriage, try to hang in there. You have a good chance of working things out. Again, don't give up too soon.

Before you make a drastic move to end a relationship, consider that you may be losing an opportunity to sharpen yourself against the hard stone of this problem. To walk away without using the problem as an opportunity to change yourself might be a serious loss. This problem may be one of the best things that ever happened to you, because it forces you into a self-examination you would not otherwise consider.

> *I am not suggesting*
> *that you draw on reserves of strength*
> *so that you can tolerate any abuse.*
> *You have probably already tolerated too much.*

Keeping your mental balance is essential. The wounded Messie who sees change coming his way has the ability to make you think that it is *you* who is wrong for wanting any change. He knows how to push your buttons. He might threaten and intimidate. Messies will attack, confuse, and throw emotional dust into the air, not because they are malicious people, but because they are trying to keep things from changing. Their best defense is to try to get you to react and become part of their emotional outburst. If they can do that, they have a chance to get you off track. If they can get you caught up in the craziness of reaction, you will not change, and they will be safer.

Sometimes, however, there is a more sinister tone to

the interplay. Messies attack, confuse, and throw dust in the air as a form of control. They see you becoming more capable of meeting your own needs, and they want to block that. They want a relationship in which your needs are totally subjugated to theirs. They deny that you have any say in how the house should look or work. They put down your feelings of unhappiness with the mess and tell you that you should not feel the way you feel. They turn to verbal abuse as a part of their power play.

You feel confused and shocked by this turn of events. Maybe you even feel guilty—that you are the source of the trouble, that you should never have asked for a nicer house. If you feel this way when you are being abused by the mess and by the personal attacks against your desire to change it, you have bought into their control-based way of running this relationship.

Rudyard Kipling wrote a poem of advice to his son. It is titled "If," and part of it reads,

> If you can keep your head when all about you
>   Are losing theirs and blaming it on you;
>   . . . you'll be a Man, my son!

In times of confusion and upset, try to keep your head by detaching emotionally in whatever way you can. Think of a beautiful picture that captures what you want for your home. Leave the house for a while. Or just change the subject. Buy time so you can gain your composure by saying things like, "Well, I suppose people see things in different ways." This statement does not give up your position nor does it challenge his. It is just a neutral statement. Perhaps you could just say nothing.

Understand that I am not saying that you should live your life serenely no matter what the circumstances. I am not suggesting that you draw on reserves of strength so that you can tolerate any abuse. You have probably already tolerated too much. Just don't use that emotional strength to protect the abuser. Use it to protect yourself. It is understood, of course, that this includes removing yourself from violence. What I am suggesting is that you keep your head when all about you are losing theirs. You will be better able to figure out what to do that way.

When things are cooler, you can proceed. Remember, you do not have to win your Messie over. You do not have to win the argument. You do not have to get him to change his mind. All of that is beside the point. What you are going to do does not require your Messie's approval. You have already stepped out of the arena where you respond to his desire to keep the house junky. You have a nobler vision, a higher path to walk. But it depends on you keeping your head when others are losing theirs and blaming it on you.

Facing Some Hard Facts

Sometimes when dealing with relational problems, we face some things we wish we could ignore. If, when you state your needs about the house, your Messie reacts in a consistently and flagrantly hostile way, you may see, perhaps for the first time, that the relationship lacks the goodwill you had assumed was there. Your Messie may ignore your concerns or diminish them or attack you or in some other way state that your concerns are not important to him. Recognizing this consistently negative attitude will be sobering and saddening.

The attitude may indicate that the Messie is fighting

some deep-felt needs within himself and is frightened and confused by what is happening. If this is so but he is trying to improve in spite of it, there is hope for compromise. There will be setbacks. There will be rocky spots. But there should also be evidence of an effort to show goodwill and commitment to your needs in the relationship. As long as there is interest in improving, there is hope for a satisfactory outcome.

If that goodwill seems totally missing, however, and ill will emerges in its place, it may no longer be possible for the person who lives with the Messie to deny the seriousness of the relational problem.

Perhaps that disillusioned person is you. You may have to face the sadness of not being cherished and cared for as you had been telling yourself you were. It is hard to face the loss of dreams in relationships. You had longed for companionship, nurturing, intimacy, respect, encouragement, and friendship. Now, because of this problem with organization, things have come to a head in your thinking. You realize that there is something destructive, irrational, and chronic in the way your Messie relates to you. It's not just in relation to the condition of the house. A loving mutuality is missing.

It is up to you to evaluate how serious the situation is. The easiest thing would be to retreat to the way things were before you realized that the love you had counted on was not there. It is hard to face and grieve the loss of the dreams you had for your life.

You cannot change anyone other than yourself. You can only state your needs and live in accord with them. The other person must want to change for your sake and the sake of the relationship. But what if that person doesn't care about you or your needs?

Give it time. Give it love. But don't live with illusion. If he says he is sorry and that he loves you dearly but continues to abuse you, see that for the cover-up it is. Follow the steps you feel are reasonable and right in order to live a life that is orderly enough for you. If nothing really changes, make your decisions with a clear head in the light of the reality you face.

Chapter 10

When to Consider Intervention

Any book dealing with the subject of living with Messies would be negligent if it did not discuss dealing with the few Messies who have serious problems beyond the ordinary bounds of society's standards.

Pernicious Messiness

The neighbors called the police because Marylou, an elderly woman living alone, could not get into her house. Actually, the newspaper story says she was attempting to get in the front door but the pile of stuff at the door was so high that she got stuck. The police came and rescued Marylou. The house was condemned. The city brought in forklifts and dump trucks to get out what Marylou called her research.

Piles of junk had kept Marylou from accessing the kitchen appliances. Some "research" had been soaked by undetected leaks in the roof. I will not continue with the description. You get the idea. By the way, Marylou would not let them throw away her valuable papers. Where they hauled tons of soggy papers for storage, I do not know.

Robert's house was becoming an eyesore in his upscale neighborhood. He stored a tricycle, among other things, on the roof. The yard and house were neglected. But the neighbors did not know about the out-of-control junk inside the house—treasures Robert was lucky enough to locate on his frequent trips to the dump.

When he ran out of room in the house, Robert stored things in the empty swimming pool. Eventually rain seeped into one part of the house, and water covered his treasures, and then a part of the roof collapsed. Robert was forced by his family to move out. He was last seen at the dump sadly trying to salvage some of his items, which the new occupant was hauling away by the truckload.

Then there's the house of Ruthie. She had a husband and two boys, ages twelve and five. Her husband drove a food delivery truck. The house looked fine from the outside. The county knocked on her door checking out a report of child abuse—the five-year-old being covered with flea bites, some infected. When the social workers went in the home, they found clothes, food, dog and cat feces, papers, and so forth all over the floor, furniture, and counters. There is no use in my trying to describe the horrible litter and destruction.

Ruthie was not a collector, but she was a messer, to put it mildly. The county's concern was to help Ruthie get the house in liveable shape for a family. When asked why she kept the house like that, Ruthie surmised she was just too lazy to clean it up. Her husband was not charged with child abuse, because the court felt that the responsibility was Ruthie's.

Clara is a widow, living alone on a limited budget in a New York rent-subsidized apartment. But now the city is about to evict her. Her apartment is a trash heap, and Clara is powerless to change it. A city attorney, appalled by the possibility of Clara becoming a bag lady out on the streets, is making frantic calls on her own time trying to find how to get help for Clara.

Now, enough of the horror stories. It is highly unlikely that your situation is like these. But suppose it is. Or suppose Marylou is your aunt. Or suppose Robert is your

Intervention is a structured, loving, but confrontational meeting between the Messie and family members and friends who are concerned about the situation they see.

father-in-law. Or suppose Ruthie is your sister. Suppose you are a social worker, and Clara is your client. Perhaps you live in a situation akin to one of these messes. Perhaps you don't live with a pernicious Messie, but you are close to and concerned about one. Maybe others are also concerned, but nobody knows what to do. This next section is for you. As with every approach, you need to evaluate whether it will meet your need. In your case, a powerful approach is needed to intervene in the situation.

Intervention: The Last Resort

Intervention is an approach to consider only after you have exhausted all other possible ways to help the pernicious Messie who runs the risk of serious physical, legal, or financial problems if he continues on his path. Intervention is a structured, loving, but confrontational meeting between the Messie and family members and friends who are concerned about the situation they see.

Cora and her sisters were concerned about their brother, Hal, who lived with his wife in an incredible junk heap. For years the sisters hinted, offered help, cajoled, begged,

> *Intervention, when rightly done,*
> *can be a gift to someone in serious need*
> *whether or not it succeeds*
> *in the way you hoped it would.*

bribed, and so forth with as much fervency as they could without turning their brother completely away from them. Things only got worse. Then the youngest sister, Fran, saw a new hopelessness in Hal. He was depressed, and the mess was more than he felt he could ever turn around. The sisters feared that he was considering suicide as a way out of his intolerable living condition.

That's when the idea of intervention came to them. As members of Al-Anon they knew about the Alcoholics Anonymous (AA) approach to intervention for alcoholics. Why not, they reasoned, intervene with Hal for his addiction? They knew an AA sponsor who had led several interventions for alcoholics and decided they would use his guidance for setting up a confrontational meeting with their brother. If they did not act and the worst happened, they would never forgive themselves for not at least trying.

In the early days of treatment of alcoholics, those involved noticed that an alcoholic would not make progress until he hit bottom, until there was no place to go but up. Intervention was first used by the Johnson Institute, a facility for the treatment of alcoholics located in Minnesota, as a way to "raise the bottom" for an alcoholic so that he would go for help before his situation became so desperate that he lost everything. In other words, they attempted to stop the downward spiral before someone's life disintegrated.

Now intervention is widely used for alcoholics and is also applied in the treatment of other addictions. As you can see from the cases presented at the beginning of this chapter, pernicious Messies may be heading for their "bottom," where they lose their homes, their families, and/or their jobs. Hal's life was in danger. In such serious cases, when all other avenues have been tried, intervention may be an acceptable tool.

Let me reemphasize that intervention is a serious step. It is a significant invasion of another person's life. It can have strong consequences in the lives of the Messie and in the lives of the intervenors if it fails. An intervention that fails may or may not have long-term negative repercussions. But intervention, when rightly done, can be a gift to someone in serious need whether or not it succeeds in the way you hoped it would.

Don't Go It Alone

Interventions must always be done under the supervision of an experienced professional. To find such a person, contact a local hospital with a unit for the treatment of addictions. If a professional has not worked with pernicious Messies before, he or she may need to be educated on the seriousness of the issue before understanding his or her place in helping with your intervention. People who are unaware of the facts may think messiness is funny in a way similar to the way people used to laugh at the antics of drunks. It is not funny when the facts are known. Intervention in the lives of pernicious Messies is uncharted territory, but it is one well worth investigating if your situation is serious and you have no place else to turn.

How Intervention Works

To prepare for an intervention, the caring family and friends meet together so that each person can clarify his or her contribution to the confrontational meeting with the group and the Messie. When ready, the group prepares to meet with the Messie, who has been unaware of the process in progress.

In the intervention meeting, in a nonjudgmental way each person details personal observations, concerns, and

> *Intervention is telling the Messie that people care, that there is help available, and that there are consequences if help is not sought.*

feelings about the situation, the effect it is having on him, and the consequences the person is willing to carry out if the Messie does not seek help in overcoming the problem. The person intervening should never mention a consequence that he is not willing to carry out. All of this is serious business and is carried out in prescribed steps.

The intervention meeting pressures the Messie to change. It is meant to precipitate a crisis in the life of the Messie by bringing out into the open all of these things that had been ignored or hidden. It serves notice that the family and friends are unified in their stand that they will no longer support the behavior that is hurting this person they care about. If the Messie continues to pursue that way of life, the family will lovingly let the consequences come to the Messie.

The group must offer a definite alternative for the Messie, some way to get treatment. Since there are so few areas developed for the treatment of this problem, the best alternative for a Messie is probably to get him to a behavioral counselor or psychologist trained in the area of addictive behavior and/or obsessive-compulsive disorders. Perhaps you will have other alternatives to use along with such treatment, such as the use of a professional organizer (see chapter 11.) In some areas Messies Anonymous support groups or obsessive-compulsive-disorder support groups are available.

Perhaps the group will feel that it is necessary for the Messie to move out of the house until it is in order. In this case, you should have a place lined up for the Messie to stay while the house is tackled. Perhaps you will have a cleaning crew ready. All of these alternatives need to be in place as possibilities in advance of the intervention to give the Messie treatment options.

Intervention is a gift given to the Messie. It is to be done with respect and caring. Intervention is not a time of blaming. Intervention is a good time for the family and friends to adopt the disease approach to the problem. We do not blame a person for having a disease, let's say diabetes. But we would expect the diabetic to seek help in knowing how to control the condition. We would expect him to cooperate with that help. Not to do so is irresponsible and harmful to the Messie and impacts negatively on the family and friends involved. Intervention is telling the Messie that people care, that there is help available, and that there are consequences if help is not sought.

Intervention is no guarantee that things will improve. If the Messie chooses recovery, wonderful. Only the Messie can do that for herself. Or the Messie may reject the whole thing. She may walk out on you. That is, of course, her choice. The family and friends have done their best to turn up the heat on the Messie so that she will face the problem and its consequences before life gets worse for her. That is all friends can do. Whether the intervention fails or succeeds, they need to pursue their own healing, their own strengthening.

Chapter 11

A Word to Professional Organizers
(To Be Read by Family
and Friends as Well)

Note to family and friends: This chapter was written to
professional organizers. However, I encourage family and
friends to read it as well for several reasons.

The first is that it will acquaint you with the work and
concerns of professional organizers. They are a group of
professionals who work for homes and businesses in an
organizational capacity. Although I belong to the National
Association of Professional Organizers (NAPO), I do not
do hands-on organizing as most professional organizers

do because I lack that kind of helping ability. I do what I do best, educate and motivate. Most organizers, however, come into the home or business and do hands-on organizing such as setting up files and developing organizational systems. They help the client decide what to get rid of, encourage them to do it, and help them store what the client decides to keep. They do not do it for the client nor do they force the client to do anything they aren't comfortable with. They are to organizing what interior decorators are to decorating.

The second reason I encourage family and friends to read this section is because it contains information that is not given in any other part of the book concerning ways you can be of help in getting additional help for your Messie.

As a member of the National Association of Professional Organizers (NAPO), I wish to say a word to those who possess the gift of organizing and have honed their skills to the level of a professional. Some of these are members of NAPO. Some are not. Whatever your affiliation, you possess a wonderful gift that those of us who are disorganized by nature appreciate and can benefit from.

As a Messie, I can tell you the path to order is fraught with dangers for the Messie. If you've been in business long, you've seen the Messie step on some of these land mines. But you might be able to help the Messie bypass the dangers better after reading this chapter.

Danger Ahead

The primary danger, which you as a professional organizer must guard against, is that the Messie might turn his focus to the wrong thing—the house and not his own internal attitudes. He may just want you to come in and "fix it." It is very easy to decide that the house is the problem; after all, that is where the pain is felt. For the Messie, however, the house is not the problem. It is only the symptom

> *Many Messies live with fear and confusion associated with their belongings.*

of the problem that resides within the Messie's way of feeling and thinking. If you as a professional organizer get the house shipshape with a place for everything and everything in its place, it will drift back to the way it was unless the Messie who is left to administer the order you have created becomes different in the process of changing the house.

You are not a psychologist, nor should you attempt to be. That is not your area of expertise. You should not spend time with the Messie analyzing why or how the problem began. The Messie you are working with may wish to discuss these underlying causes with you. After all, you are probably the first person with whom he has felt free to expose this personal and humiliating part of himself. Simply by taking this job you have become intimate with him. So for this reason you may find that your client talks to you in depth about his feelings about the problem.

What's more, you will be dealing with personal aspects of his life. Bills, correspondence, and receipts tell a lot about a person—things one would not ordinarily share with a stranger. Many are even reluctant to share these things with a mental health professional. But because you are in the home or office, on his turf and working with his papers, he may be open with you—even about fears.

Many Messies live with fear and confusion associated with their belongings. They fear getting rid of things. If they do, they will lose part of their past or expose themselves to the danger of not having what they need in the future. They use their things to define themselves. When a woman gets rid of her maternity clothes, for instance, she is throwing away an important part of her womanhood. The messiness may symbolize a creative spirit that defines someone as an *artiste*. If he gives up the symbol, will he lose his identity or his muse? Possessions can reflect dreams, hopes, interests, hobbies, and causes, all of which the Messie will be sharing with you. All of this puts you in a position where you will have to exercise professionalism and avoid becoming something you were never meant to be—a psychologist, a close buddy, or an adopted family member.

On top of this and compounding the problem, some professional organizers may enjoy the counselor role. The instant intimacy is pleasant to them. They like to sit and talk about the *whys* and *wherefores* of the problem. The clients seem to need it. Some clients may even wish to use you as an inexpensive therapist. Some may think it is dangerous to try to make external change before they know the psychological aspects of the problem; they're afraid the change might scar their psyches. They feel you understand mess; it's your expertise.

Some would even prefer to talk about the house and their feelings toward it than to begin the hard job of working on the house. They use talking as a stalling device; anything would be better than biting the bullet and getting to work.

You see, a pseudotherapeutic relationship is an easy situation for the professional organizer to drift into. But it is not your training or calling.

Your Stance

Since you realize that the house is not the real problem and since you are aware that you are not a mental health professional, what can you do to best serve the interests of your client? Much can be done if you keep your focus.

- Assure the Messie that she is not alone, that there are many people who struggle with the problem of clutter and disorganization.

- Provide a standard for what is normal. Many Messies do not realize that most people do not keep all of their old water bills for years back. They do not keep all of Johnny's baby shoes. You have an advantage that will work to the benefit of the Messie. You are an expert. You can use that fact as a strong influence on the thinking of the Messie.

- Offer encouragement. What the Messie is doing is very hard for her. She is confronting fears, habits, and ingrained ways of thinking. She is touching something very deep inside of herself. She has used these items to provide safety and comfort. Now she is left exposed without protection. For the most part, she is pretty much unaware of how much she has used these things to ward off fear. All she knows is that she feels very uncomfortable when getting rid of this stuff.

- Even if the Messie falters and fails, maybe by pulling a discarded item out of the garbage, remind her that at one time she had not been willing to throw anything away. She is making progress. It goes without saying that harsh and judgmental comments do not belong in this situation.

- Extend compliments. Messies are ashamed of the way they have let things go. They may think that you won't like them if you see this aspect. Your nonjudgmental attitude coupled with an occasional genuine compliment will help to assuage that fear. One professional organizer I know was looking for something to compliment in a client and chose the person's sense of balance: Not many people would be able to stack piles of paper so high without them falling down.

  Looking for positives to compliment will help to keep you in the right frame of mind. Working with a fearful client facing such a challenging task requires patience. If you do not keep a positive attitude, you will tend to lose your professional objectivity.

- Keep the tension down. Without making light of the problem, have a sense of humor. This is a very tense activity for the Messie. By having an upbeat attitude, you can help break the tension. You may also wish to have the client's favorite music or a TV on in the background as a distraction. When I first started taking control of my clutter, I turned the television on to lighten the intensity of what I was starting to do. I was alone, however. You will have to evaluate the usefulness of television in your setting.

Challenge Actions

Now to the actual activity. If the real problem is the Messie's thoughts and feelings and if you are not a counselor digging up the root of the problem, how then can you help the client to get to that root? Permanent change can occur as you challenge her thoughts and feelings by action. It is easy enough to talk about change, but talk is tested as it is challenged by doing. Does the person really

> *Couch the goals in terms of dreams.*
> *To speak of goals puts too much*
> *pressure on some Messies.*

want to change? Obviously, she has already begun the process of change or she would not have called you in the first place. Only by continuing the process will her true resolve be known. You can help by structuring her efforts and offering support.

Help Clarify the Client's Goals

Couch the goals in terms of dreams. To speak of goals puts too much pressure on some Messies. They may say that they wish to (a) get rid of stuff, (b) organize what they keep, (c) have a neat house so they can live a better life (i.e., sit down at the table without moving things or sleep on a bed not filled with books and clothes). Probably they will not dare to dream beyond the practical. Few Messies express the highest dream of all—that they could have a beautiful home and entertain friends graciously. This they dare not hope at first.

Make goals concrete by helping them find pictures of how they dream their house will look. Suggest they keep those pictures in view. When they wane in their resolve, that picture of how the house can look along with a review of how their new decisions fit into that dream can spur the Messie on. It's easier to throw things away and reorganize when you remember the reason you're going to all the trouble.

Help Plan Rewards

Everyone needs to have concrete recognition of personal efforts. At first make the rewards for small victories, maybe sticking at a task for a whole hour. Later adjust for bigger projects. Before you begin a task, decide what will be the reward when it is finished. It could be an expensive lipstick, a piece of costume jewelry, a trip to the movies, or a hot fudge sundae (nonfat yogurt and fudge sauce, of course). The reward itself is not as important as the success it signifies.

Your Part

Your part in the cleanup process is to help clients get rid of things and find appropriate storage for what is kept. What does this mean in nitty-gritty terms? You may tell them what papers need to be kept. If necessary, at first you may actually put things in the trash, but eventually they must do the job themselves. You can help them set up a file or a notebook storage system. You might direct them to books that give specific instructions for what to keep, for how long, and how to store things. Suggestions include *Getting Organized* by Stephanie Winston, *Taming the Paper Tiger* by Barbara Hemphill, and *Conquering the Paper Pile-Up* by Stephanie Culp. You may prefer to relate verbally the kind of information in these books, but it's better if you point out something in print. Messies like official things, especially if they are written. You know how much they like printed information; look how much they have snuggled around them.

Overcoming the Fear

Remember the Messie's fear: to get rid of stuff; to file it or put it in a storage system out of sight where he will not be able to find it when he needs it. The fact that he was not able to find it when he kept it in piles does not make him any less distrustful of the system you suggest.

To fight the fear, the Messie should work with your support for at least an hour, maybe two. You see, the fear decreases as the time goes by. The Messie learns that he can feel the fear and continue anyway. In other words, he becomes more comfortable with the discomfort. He learns that he does not need to be controlled by the fear. In time the fear lessens, and he is freed to control the belongings.

To track the shrinking fear, the Messie can use a helpful system of fear control. It consists of an evaluation scale of one to five. Five represents a great deal of fear, approaching panic. One represents comfort, absence of fear. The numbers in between show the graduation of fear into comfort.

1	2	3	4	5
Comfort	Some Discomfort	Moderate Discomfort	Severe Discomfort	Close to Panic

Have the Messie rate himself at the beginning of the organizational work. Every so often, maybe every fifteen minutes, he should rate himself again. If you sense his comfort level changing dramatically at some point, have him rate himself (whether or not it is the scheduled time to do so) adding a notation about what precipitated the drastic change. This tracking will sensitize the Messie to his own feelings in a more or less objective way. When the Messie quantifies fear by giving it a number, it seems more manageable. It seems like something apart from himself over which he has some control. By doing this, the Messie begins to see progress in his feelings. If things go well, fear will begin to diminish as it is confronted.

You can see from this exercise how the actual activity of organizing confronts the thinking and feeling of the Messie. Your presence in a nonjudgmental and supportive role enables the Messie to find the courage to do the confronting.

There's More

This does not mean things will always go smoothly. If you help the Messie store something and she can't use the retrieval system you have helped set up, she may become angry or frightened—probably both. Actually, she may more or less deliberately not find something so she can feel distrustful of your system and have an excuse for not continuing.

If the Messie gets angry at you or at your system, do not get caught up in the anger. Remind the Messie that you are working on goals that both of you agreed on. If the anger continues, tell the Messie that you understand that it is frustrating. Do not try to continue. Say that you will resume when things are better. If the anger recurs, consider recommending another person to help the Messie with the problem. If the Messie cannot maintain a working relationship with any helper after several tries, he should consider receiving professional help from a psychologist who specializes in behavioral therapy.

Final Words

Two final words are necessary. First, it is not a good idea to have several people working with the Messie as he works to get control. However, you may wish to find a friend or a family member who is able to work in a detached way with the Messie when you are not present. Hiring a professional organizer is expensive. If the project is huge, the cost of long-range help can be prohibitive. As an alternative, you, as a professional, might act as a coach who sets up a working schedule and supervises goals. You might work with the Messie and the family helper on a weekly basis to check in on the progress. As the Messie works with the friend or family member and gets to the point where storage is necessary, you can help set up the storage systems.

This method of using a helper also makes it more clear to the Messie that, in the end, no fairy godmother in the guise of a professional organizer is going to wave a magic wand over the house and make the mess go away. Care must be taken not to take over the project or to let the helper do so. Always the Messie carries the responsibility. You are just part of her meeting that responsibility.

Sometimes a friend or family member can act as the Messie's sole helper—if the desire for change is strong in the Messie and the helper is objective. However, because of the emotional overlay of this problem and the confusion it causes, objective outside help is invaluable.

The second help you may wish to suggest for your client is in the form of a behavioral therapist. If things are not going well in your organizational work, you may indicate that in this case you feel that the help of a behavioral therapist is needed. Your client may have a full-blown obsessive-compulsive disorder (OCD) beyond your area of expertise. Locating behavioral therapists who have experience in this area is a service to your clients. You may wish to contact the Association for the Advancement of Behavior Therapy (15 West Thirty-Sixth

Street, New York, NY 10018) to find out if a particular therapist is a member and if the member lists OCD as a specialty. The Anxiety Disorders Association (6000 Executive Boulevard, Suite 200, Rockville, MD 20852) will also provide the names of behavior therapists in your area who treat OCD.

For more information, see books on OCD, including *Getting Control: Overcoming Your Obsessions and Compulsions* by Lee Baer which I have found very helpful.

If the Messie does not have an OCD, but you feel a therapist would be helpful, two other branches of psychology that deal with behavior changes are behavior modification and reality therapy. In my experience, introspective therapy, which emphasizes childhood experiences, has not been very effective in helping problems with clutter. Call your local psychological association to locate a behavior oriented therapist.

Chapter 12

Let Me Ask You...

Paula's Story

Paula works hard at a wholesale nursery all day and returns daily to her two young children and her husband who also works full time. When her husband's schedule allows him to be at home with the children, he doesn't do dishes or pick up. He's too tired, and the children are troublesome. Of course when she is home, she, in spite of tiredness and troublesome children, manages to get things done. Paula wants to return to college to better herself, but too much work and too little help are major obstacles. She doesn't know how she can go to college with the two little ones. She doesn't want to ask her in-laws to help. They have already raised their children and deserve a rest, she reasons. There's another problem of not enough money for college. Because nobody is in charge of the finances, checks are bouncing.

In frustration, Paula wants to give away her children and husband too. She needs more help than she is getting. She threatens to leave clothes all over the house where they are dropped. She also threatens to stop washing any dishes so her husband won't be able to find a clean plate to eat from. Perhaps that will get his attention.

Let me ask you, Paula, what are you going to do about your situation? Rather than taking the radical and emotional approaches that flit to mind in times of stress, can you think of any alternatives you could use to improve your life?

Perhaps Paula has some inkling of her options. She can break her own rule and approach her in-laws for help with the children. She can go to the consumer credit counseling service for financial advice. Her county has an active mental health facility where she can ask for counsel to help her sort out her alternatives. She can quit saying it is impossible to go back to school and can actually apply for fellowships and loans to see what the costs will be. Perhaps a friend from the church can give her some support.

One thing is certain: She needs to start doing something different.

After she has sorted out her alternatives, she can talk again to her husband, but this time with a difference. There is no need for begging. This time she comes with dignity and resolve. She will not come with talk only. She will come with actions. She needs to set her bottom line, make specific her action plan, and figure her options in case it does not work. He may change; he may not.

Suppose he will not. What will she do for herself to accomplish her goals?

Rachel

What will Rachel do? Her whole family is messy. Well, not quite the whole family. She has five adult children and stepchildren living with her. Three of the adult children are Messies, as is her husband. They have a large house, but not large enough to keep the clutter of the four Messies at bay.

Rachel manages to keep the living room and other public areas in order so she is not embarrassed if someone stops by. She keeps the doors to the children's rooms closed. Years ago she used the reward system and tried to change them, but she gave up on that approach and went to the closed doors. This frustrates her because she likes open spaces and is unhappy about the necessity to close off the disorganized spaces.

At night she sneaks into the bathroom of her grown children and cleans it so that they won't know that she is still taking care of them. She hopes that each one will think that another sibling did it. She is concerned that her mother will see the children's bedrooms and look down on her. Her husband leaves books, papers, and assorted junk out on his side of the bedroom, and this ruins the visual aspect of the order and beauty she maintains on her side.

Recently, one of Rachel's daughters moved out, taking her furniture and vacating a room near Rachel's bedroom. Rachel immediately commandeered it for her office, her own private room, a place in which she could make things lovely. The next week her daughter, who was the messiest of all the children, decided to move back home again.

Rachel reread the important parts of her well-marked book *The Dance of Anger: A Woman's Guide to Changing the Patterns of Intimate Relationships* by Harriet Lerner.

Then she made a decision, one of the hardest she had ever made, she said. She asked her daughter to take a smaller room in a more distant part of the house. The daughter, not much in tune with her surroundings anyway, could not care less which room she had and moved into the other room contentedly. In her special room that night Rachel secretly danced with joy.

Now, what will you do, Rachel? Will you keep struggling on with things pretty much the way they are, leaving the house and relationships where they have been, sneaking around to clean up where you must, sacrificing well-being because of the clutter that exists behind the lines of demarcation? Or will your success in your bold move encourage you to take further charge of your own life? Perhaps you will let vegetables grow on the ring around the bathtub and let the pile of wet towels grow high to the ceiling if the family doesn't take an interest in cleaning up themselves. Or perhaps you have things pretty well under control and feel you have done enough changing for a while. It could be that your new room will give you the space you feel you need so that you can live with the mess in your bedroom. Only you can decide that.

But let me ask you one more question. If you were to make one more change, Rachel, what might it be? Think about it for a while, and then decide if and when you will make that change.

Bob

Let me ask a few questions of Bob, whose wife, Vivian, is dreamy and disturbed. She cries often, stays in bed a lot, and is seeing a therapist. Bob cares deeply about Vivian.

Her mental health seems so fragile that he does everything he can to keep the pressure of the terribly muddled house from disturbing her. But he is losing the battle. She needs to keep everything. She becomes frightened if anything leaves her possession. She wants it sitting out where it can assure her that it is there for her. Perhaps a new therapist would be the answer, Bob surmises.

What are your options, Bob? Only you can know. Can you, like Rachel, find a spot in the house that is yours alone where you can create order? Are you going to accommodate your whole personal life to your wife's weakness, or can you find activities outside the home that will strengthen you for the time when you are at home? Should you begin seeing a counselor for yourself or join a support group where you can find group help in deciding what to do? Should you go on bravely holding up more than your end and saying nothing, or can you share your feelings of hurt and disappointment with her? Should you discuss the situation dispassionately with her? Or is there some other alternative?

Plan of Action

Throughout the book we've discussed a plan of action. But let's set it down clearly. What can Paula or Bob or Rachel or you do to move out of the status quo?

1. Face the Facts of How Serious Things Are

Denial is a big part of problems like this. Perhaps because the mess developed so slowly over such a long time, you got used to it and now deny how bad things are.

2. Get a Vision for How Things Can Be

Perhaps you need to realize that God did not intend for you to live like this when he put you on the earth.

Catch a glimpse of how happy and useful you could be without this albatross around your neck.

3. Take a Step to Get Help

This book is one step. You need to decide what other help you need. Here are some specific possibilities you might consider.

- Attend self-help, support-group meetings. Groups offer powerful support. There is nothing quite like being with people who really understand what you are going through. They are free and available in most areas of the country. Many twelve-step groups deal with your situation. These are not groups where people sit around and complain about their problems or the people causing the problems. People who attend the groups keep the focus on themselves and how they can live more vibrant and fulfilling lives, no matter what their circumstances (see table).

- Consider therapy, if appropriate. Some things are hard to identify and deal with on our own. Sometimes we may need the guidance of a professional to help us untangle the confusion of the problem and evaluate solutions. Counselors who can offer you the kind of help you are looking for will often identify themselves in terms of *codependency* issues.

- Read other books. Many good books are available. I've included an annotated bibliography at the end of the book to give you pointers for where to start reading.

- Attend seminars and workshops. Once you tune into solving a problem, it is amazing how quickly you spot functions that address that problem.

Support Groups

CODA	A group for codependents—the fixers, enablers, or helper personalities who tend to step in and compensate for someone else not taking responsibility for himself or herself.
Al-Anon	If alcohol is or has been involved in your life—if your parent, child, spouse, or friend has an alcohol problem, even if it is not something you are struggling with at this point—Al-Anon is a good place for you to address those life complications.
Parents Anonymous	If your child is a problem, this group may be helpful for you.
Local Listings	Try the phone book to track down groups in your area. Some groups may announce meetings in your local newspaper. Or write to: American Self-Help Clearinghouse, Saint Clares-Riverside Medical Center, Pocono Road, Denville, NJ 07834.
M-Anon	These groups deal directly with the problem of living with a Messie. At this writing, the group is in development stages. For a free introductory newsletter, to find out if there is a group near you, or to start a group, write to: M-Anon, 5025 SW 114 Avenue, Miami, FL 33165. Starting a group is very easy, and the advantage of starting your own group is that you can choose a location and time convenient to your schedule. (Note: Messies Anonymous is for the Messie; M-Anon is for the MessieMate.)

Take a step to get help. Perhaps it will be getting up the courage to tell one other person how bad things are. For someone in another phase it might mean contacting someone to help with an intervention. For too long you've tried doing it all on your own and it hasn't worked. Now reach out for help.

4. Stop Taking Care of the Messie

Just because you have his best good in mind does not mean you offer help inappropriately. For the most part, this means doing nothing to manipulate the Messie. Don't praise accomplishments so he will keep going in the right direction. Don't criticize, hoping to push him into order. Don't protect him by adjusting your life to the limitations of his problem. For example, invite people over to the house. Let the Messie face the impact of their disapproval of his lifestyle. Let him feel the consequences of his actions whether good or bad.

5. Take Care of Yourself

Taking your focus off the Messie kicks up a lot of personal issues that have remained covered over. As you focus on yourself, you may see that the unhealthy way you related to the Messie is just one of the unhealthy weeds in your life. Those weeds have to be uprooted. New and beautiful plants need to replace them. What are those new plants? Only you know the aspects of yourself that have been neglected because of the Messie problem. Friends have been neglected or not made. Perhaps you will look for a job or quit one or start a hobby or go back to school. Perhaps you have kept yourself busy with activities because it kept you from the house and dulled you to the seriousness of your problem. Maybe you will keep those activities but with a new awareness of their contribution to the balance of your life.

I recently tore a fingernail while out and dropped by to see a manicurist. When she got out some glue and powder and set to work, I expressed surprise that such repair technique was available.

"You don't pamper yourself much, do you?" she asked.

"Well, I guess maybe not."

"You should. If we take good care of ourselves, we can take better care of others."

How true. Those of us whose way of life is to focus on others tend to neglect ourselves unnecessarily. It is not a healthy way to live.

I have a friend who tried to break herself of her habitual self-neglect. She had developed unhealthy rules about her own care. For one, she bought clothes only on sale. This meant that some clothes she really liked, she

> *This has been a book about love.*
> *And about honesty. And probably about courage.*

never got. She bought other clothes she didn't care much for—because they were on the sale rack. (In her circumstances, money was not really an issue.) She began to see that she didn't think she was worth full-price clothes. To challenge this thinking and this way of life, she forced herself to go to the store and buy a full-price dress. That money was well spent, because it ushered in a necessary change in her outlook.

Is all of this selfish? Yes, in a wholesome way. You are finally taking yourself seriously and allowing life to blossom.

6. Make Your Plans and Follow Them

Many suggestions have been made in this book—from how to first confront a Messie to how to conduct an intervention. Much of this involves your deciding exactly what you want changed. Go back through the book and decide exactly where you want to go and how you want to get there. Write down a plan in one-two-three fashion, and then get started. *Always evaluate and adjust as you go but never lose your vision.*

Love, Honesty, and Courage

This has been a book about love. And about honesty. And probably about courage. It is a book about love because it asks you to quit neglecting yourself and to act in a lovingly responsible way to meet your own needs. It also asks you to lovingly accept the Messie in your life as the person he is, even at his worst.

It is a book about honesty because it asks you to quit denying that the problem is as bad as it is or that it affects you as negatively as it does. It asks you to stop denying the impact of the disorder on your social life, your emotional life, and your relationship. Perhaps it asks you to take that generalized anger and frustration you have been feeling in your relationship and put it smack dab where it belongs—on the problem of clutter. Most difficult of all, it asks you to look at your part in the problem. Has there been some overlooked and hidden payoff for you in the house being a mess? Have you unwittingly allowed it—or even encouraged it?

It also takes courage. Old, familiar habits, no matter how hurtful they are to us, are somehow satisfying. Uprooting them is about as hard as having a molar pulled

—and just about as pleasant. It will take months to replace the old habits of carping, resentment, anger, challenge, power plays, and helping with new attitudes of responsible living. It will take courage to challenge our thinking. Where we thought we had power, we do not. Where we thought we were powerless, we are not. We were accepting when we should have been bold. Or pushy in areas that were none of our business. All of this takes time to see and correct. We will fail, make mistakes, correct them, and fail again. We need patience with ourselves and our Messies. Perhaps we will need support, maybe with a behavioral therapist. A reality therapist would also be good. It is our responsibility to do whatever it takes to get the job done, the job of taking care of our responsibilities for ourselves, giving the Messie that same privilege, and nurturing the relationship in the process.

A big order? Yes, but whoever said that good things come easy? It is called living. I am not talking about hard, bite-the-bullet living. I am talking about zingy, honest, invigorating, glad-to-be-alive living. The time has come to stop hiding from longings, problems, or our authentic selves. That takes courage, but it is the only way to open ourselves to abundant life.

Freedom

This is also a book about freedom—the freedom of letting go of trying to exert power over others. It is about the freedom of claiming our own personal power. It is leaving behind coercion and embracing personal responsibility.

Nothing is so imprisoning as the bondage of the rules we used to follow. We had to make sure we were perfect in our own rigid interpretation of perfection. We had to try to manipulate others into our way of behavior—in love, we told ourselves, and we hoped without their realizing it. We denied our own feelings. Some of us used our struggle with the problem to divert us from facing our own pain. In short, we were avoiding life and didn't even realize it. Letting go of all of that is emancipating.

We will express our needs and confront where necessary our irresponsible behavior, but we do not take responsibility for changing our Messies. We don't rescue them anymore or indulge in caretaking. We are through with that. What they do about changing, or not changing, is their own business. What we do about their changing or lack of changing is our business. It is as simple as that.

Sharing from a Full Cup

Let me urge you to give less attention to the problem and more to the business of living fully. Nothing is so compelling to encourage others toward rational living than the presence of a healthy and vibrant force in the home. As you turn your energies away from the struggle of this problem and toward strengthening yourself in body, soul, and spirit, you may be surprised at the influence you have. Turn your energies toward developing love toward your Messie and, where appropriate, intimacy in the relationship.

Finally, turn your eyes toward God from whom flows true life—in this world and in the one to come. Any person, believer or not, can benefit from leaving behind the bondage of trying to control others. An added grace comes to those who seek the One who is the source of all health.

Some people have a compartmentalized faith. It is like a cherry on top of a sundae—a desirable and attractive addition to but not an integral part of their lives. Others have a relationship with God that is more like vanilla extract blended into every part of the sundae and giving flavor throughout. That's the way it should be as we face the problem of the Messie and the house. If we let God into every part of our lives and relate to him as he is portrayed in the Scriptures, we find that our difficult relationships and our thorny problems are touched by his grace and graciousness.

Perhaps because we know we are well and thoroughly loved by him, we are more willing to love others when the loving gets tough. Perhaps because we know we have been forgiven and have his spirit of forgiveness living within us, we are a bit more willing to do the same. Perhaps because he lets us make our own decisions and suffer our own consequences (as he has from the beginning with Adam and Eve), we are more willing to offer that privilege to others. Somehow, because he loves and cares for us in such a gentle way, we are encouraged to treat ourselves with tender regard. He helps wisely and appropriately; we try to do so as well.

When I go to church, I enter with my family; I greet my friends; I enjoy the fellowship. However, somewhere early into the service I turn my attention from the crowd around me and to the unseen presence in our midst. I spend the hour with him until the benediction when the crowd surfaces again and that season of active fellowship with him draws to a close. But that same intimate experience with God can be a part of our daily lives, strengthening us and changing us for the better.

Jesus said, "Here I am! I stand at the door and knock. If anyone hears my voice and opens the door, I will come in and eat with him, and he with me" (Rev. 3:20 NIV). That verse reminds me of a popular painting of Jesus waiting to be let in at a door that looks as if it might be the entrance to a garden. I like to see the inner self as a garden. No matter how well we cultivate that garden of our

> *God hath not given us the spirit of fear;*
> *but of power, and of love, and of a sound mind*
> *(2 Tim. 1:7).*

spirits, we are left unfulfilled until that day when we realize, whether all at once or by degrees, the purpose of the garden. The garden is a meeting place, a place of fellowship—as it has been from the beginning of time when God walked and talked with his first creation in Eden, the first garden, in the cool of the evening.

Now the millennia have rolled by, and it is our turn to invite him into our heart's garden and walk with him there. For forgiveness. For renewal. For nourishment. For love that will blossom and inspire others to want what we have.

I know that this is a book about housekeeping. I realize that it speaks about solving difficult relationship problems. I am very aware that I have encouraged you to cherish and take care of yourself while loving others well. But just trying harder won't cut it. It's just too complex and too hard to do alone. We don't even know our real needs, much less the way to meet them. When we have done the best we can with ourselves and our relationships, it is time to turn inward and realize that there are some things that can be fulfilled only by a relationship with God.

So we go to the garden of our hearts, and we invite him in. We walk and we talk. We receive his strength and guidance. We fail, and we seek forgiveness. We learn, and we grow. But never do we grow beyond our need for his care and the courage he provides.

Grant Me Courage

Time after time the Bible says, "Fear not." And 2 Timothy 1:7 is a powerful promise: "God hath not given us the spirit of fear; but of power, and of love, and of a sound mind" (KJV).

It takes courage to change. I have used the word *fear* frequently when talking about Messies, but it applies to you, the MessieMate, too. That fear keeps you from moving out of your situation. When you stay the same, you protect the Messie from having to face his own sickness.

However, it is not for the Messie that you stay the same. It is for yourself, to protect yourself from taking responsibility for a new way of life. Although you may hate it, you have grown comfortable living the way you do. It always seems easier to stay sick than to take the risk of getting well. You are ashamed to admit how the house is, afraid to challenge the Messie, fearful of taking action that might upset your relationship.

I used to ride a merry-go-round with a brass ring—just out of easy reach—that one could grab by stretching as far as possible out from the racing horse. I was a child. My arms were short. It took a lot of courage to get an outside horse, set my eye on that brass ring, and take the chance of falling off the moving merry-go-round as I reached out dangerously far for the ring. I don't know what the prize was for the person who grabbed the ring. I don't even recall whether I actually got a ring. All I clearly remember is that I dared to try.

For Pete's sake (no, for your own sake and everyone else's), take courage to get on the merry-go-round of your own life. Grab an outside horse and stretch courageously outward. It is scary, I'll grant you. There is danger involved. But it is worthwhile knowing you were not willing to just stand there and watch it go around without you.

You may need to change your attitudes, your feelings, your ambitions, and whatever else hinders you from building your world into the beautiful and orderly world you dream could be yours.

The Builder

An elderly carpenter was ready to retire. He told his employer-contractor of his plans to leave the house-building business and live a more leisurely life with his wife enjoying his extended family. He would miss the paycheck, but he needed to retire. They could get by.

The contractor was sorry to see his good worker go and asked if he could build just one more house as a personal favor. The carpenter said *yes,* but in time it was easy to see that his heart was not in his work. He resorted to shoddy workmanship and used inferior materials. It was an unfortunate way to end his career.

When the carpenter finished his work and the builder came to inspect the house, the contractor handed the front-door key to the carpenter. "This is your house," he said, "my gift to you."

What a shock! What a shame! If he had only known he was building his own house, he would have done it all so differently. Now he had to live in the home he had built none too well.

So it is with us. We build our lives in a distracted way, reacting rather than acting, willing to put up less than the best. At important points we do not give the job our best effort. Then with a shock we look at the situation we have created and find that we are now living in the house we have built. If we had realized, we would have done it differently.

Fortunately, it is possible to change our habits. Each change of action will have an impact on how your life is built. It is not easy, but it is possible. Your Messie will fight the change in you. More surprisingly and more subtly, you will resist changing without even realizing what you are doing. You think that if you continue what you have been doing all along that has not worked, one of these days things *should* work differently. You think you will try just once more using your previous way of handling the Messie and the mess. But it will never work. When you keep doing the same thing, you keep getting the same results. That is a law of nature.

Think of yourself as the carpenter. Think about your house. Each day you hammer a nail, place a board, or erect a wall. Build wisely. It is the only life you will ever build. Even if you live it for only one day more, that day deserves to be lived graciously and with dignity. The plaque on the wall says, "Life is a do-it-yourself project."

"Nobody else can walk it for you," says the spiritual.

"The buck stops here," said the sign on President Truman's desk.

Who could say it more clearly? Your life today is the result of your attitudes and choices in the past. Your life tomorrow will be the result of your attitudes and the choices you make today.

Let me ask you, what are you going to do?

Annotated Bibliography

I suppose it is understood that all annotated bibliographies are a reflection of personal opinion. That is certainly the case in this instance. Hundreds of books on the shelves of stores and libraries might be useful to you. This is both a blessing and a curse. Because readers are blessed with so many, the seeker is cursed with the enormous task of making an appropriate choice. To provide some guidance in this confusion and to give credit for helpful insights, I here mention some of the books that have provided background for this book.

As you seek some of these resources in a bookstore or library, look at the other books clustered in that area. You might like some of these sister books better than the ones I mention. Of course, if you really want a particular book, you can always ask a store to order it for you. If it is out of print, a library search might help you. And, interestingly enough, I have found some of my most helpful books browsing around in secondhand bookstores.

There is not much material out there relating directly to the subject of this book—the problem of living with a disorganized person. In fact, I have found nothing. I have perused a broad range of material to add to my experience with chronically disorganized people.

I want to mention that I do not endorse *all* of the ideas in the books I recommend. My personal convictions often disagree with modern written consensus. Yet I do not have to agree with everything to find a kernel of truth that is helpful to me. For those ideas I am grateful. I leave it to the reader to discern which ideas to value and which to discard.

Very Valuable Books

Beattie, Melody. *Codependent No More.* New York: Harper & Row, 1980.

——. *Beyond Codependency.* San Francisco: Harper & Row, 1989. Classics dealing with the kind of relationships I have discussed in this book. She writes with warmth and insight.

Baer, Lee. *Getting Control: Overcoming Your Obsessions and Compulsions.* Boston: Little, Brown and Company, 1991. A valuable help for persons with obsessive-compulsive disorders. Most does not deal with clutter, but the principles apply. Deals with diagnosis and treatment.

Dobson, James. *Love Must Be Tough: New Hope for Families in Crisis.* Dallas: Word Inc., 1983. Practical and direct. Dobson delivers the kind of reliable help he is noted for. Written from a Christian perspective for women with difficult husbands.

Groom, Nancy. *From Bondage to Bonding: Escaping Codependency, Embracing Biblical Love.* Colorado Springs: NavPress, 1991. This book deals in more depth with intimacy (bonding) than any book I know. Moving and helpful insights on the grace of God supporting the seeker in this scary pursuit.

Lehmkuhl, Dorothy, and **Dolores Cotter Lamping.** *Organizing for the Creative Person: Mastering Time and Reaching Your Goals.* New York: Crown, 1993. A collaboration of an in-the-field, hands-on organizer and a psychotherapist who really know their stuff. Offers insights and practical helps that will prove invaluable in understanding those creative, right-brained disorganized people we call Messies. This book emphasizes finding one's own organizational style and learning to live with it. If you are an organized person, the book will help you because it emphasizes the differences between the way organized (left-brained) and disorganized (right-brained) people relate to the pursuit of order.

Lerner, Harriet Goldhor. *The Dance of Anger: A Woman's Guide to Changing the Patterns of Intimate Relationships.* New York: Harper & Row, 1985. Explains clearly how relationships work and how they can be improved. Despite the title, it takes a reasonable and moderate approach.

Norwood, Robin. *Women Who Love Too Much, When You Keep Wishing and Hoping He'll Change.* New York: Pocket Books, 1985. An excellent book (one of the best) on the subject of difficult relationships, why some women have them and some don't, how to deal with them once you are in them, and how to avoid them in the future. Very insightful and practical. For some it will be a gold mine of help. I found it after most of this book was written, and although it does not apply directly to living with a disorganized person, it strongly confirmed the approach I had taken toward handling this difficult relationship.

Other Good Books

Bryant, Roberta Jean. *Stop Improving and Start Living.* San Rafael, Calif.: New World Library, 1991. Emphasis on creativity, freedom, joy, and well-being. Many sensible and heart-warming insights.

Dobson, James. *What Wives Wish Their Husbands Knew about Women.* Wheaton, Ill.: Tyndale House, 1975. A sensitive treatment of many issues of marriage that confront women. Dobson is the popular host of the "Focus on the Family" radio program.

Dowling, Colette. *The Cinderella Complex.* New York: Summit Books, 1981. Cinderella was not a proactive person. She waited in the ashes for somebody else—her fairy godmother or her prince—to change her life. This book addresses the issue of responsibility for our own lives, which, rightly applied, can lead to more satisfactory relationships.

Evans, Patricia. *The Verbally Abusive Relationship.* Holbrook, Mass.: Bob Adams, 1992. Excellent book. *Newsweek* called it "a ground breaking new book." Tops in addressing the power issues in relationships and how those are played out verbally. It would do wonders for the MessieMate who feels that the Messie in his or her life is using the clutter as a power ploy and is not interested in meeting the MessieMate's need for an orderly house.

Kiley, Dan. *What to Do When He Won't Change.* New York: G. P. Putnam's Sons, 1987. Deals with preparing yourself for improving yourself. Many specific strategies to change your life for more satisfying relationships.

Levinson, Harold N. *Total Concentration: How to Understand Attention Deficit Disorders.* New York: M. Evans and Company, Inc., 1992. This book contains a self test, treatment guidelines for you and your doctor, and a lot of helpful information about being delivered from the effects af ADD.

Peck, M. Scott. *The Road Less Traveled.* New York: Simon & Schuster, 1978. A best-selling book by a psychiatrist. Touches on love, responsibility, spiritual growth (in terms of the natural human spirit; Peck did not become a Christian until after he wrote this book), confrontation, intimacy, separateness, and many other basic human needs.

Shaevitz, Marjorie Hansen. *The Superwoman Syndrome.* New York: Warner Books, 1984. A book on taking charge of your time and life. Written for women. Includes a section by Morton Shaevitz to give the man's viewpoint.

Sterling, A. Justin. *What Really Works with Men.* New York: Warner Books, 1992. Many practical and some startling proposals. This book is right on the money when it comes to letting go of trying to control someone else (in this case the man in your life) and living your life to the full.

Stoddard, Alexandra. *Living Beautifully Together.* New York: Doubleday, 1989. A rather idyllic view of sharing a home with another. It is charming and is included here because it is nice to find the rarefied air of charm every once in a while to keep going in the midst of a problem.

Ury, William. *Getting Past No: Negotiating Your Way from Confrontation to Cooperation.* New York: Bantam, 1993. Written for the business world, it has strong application for personal negotiating.

York, Phyllis, David York, and **Ted Wachtel.** *Toughlove.* New York: Bantam, 1982. A guidebook for parents of difficult teens. Offers a much-needed perspective and is particularly valuable because of its no-nonsense and structured plan for change. It is not a mean-spirited book. A helpful guide in improving many difficult relationships. I highly recommend it.

Other Comments about Readings

It is not surprising that I recommend my own previous books, all published by Fleming H. Revell.

The Messies Manual: The Procrastinator's Guide to Good Housekeeping, 1981.

*Messies 2, New Strategies to Restoring Order in Your Life and
    Home,* 1986.

*The Messies Superguide: Strategies and Ideas for Conquering
    Catastrophic Living,* 1987.

*Messie No More: Practical Steps to Put the Messie Lifestyle
    Behind You,* 1989.

Meditations for Messies: A Guide to Order and Serenity, 1992.

All of these were written to help the Messie who wants
to improve. However, *Messie No More,* which explains
in some detail why Messies have the problem they have,
would be beneficial to the MessieMate as well as to the
Messie.

If alcohol abuse is involved in your relationship with
your Messie, disorder in the house is not your primary
problem—alcohol is. See these books:

Drews, Toby Rice. *Getting Them Sober.* South Plainfield, N.J.:
    Bridge Publishing, 1980.

Mumey, Jack. *Loving an Alcoholic.* New York: Bantam Books,
    1985.

Family cooperation, or lack thereof, can make all the
difference in success or failure. The following talk about
family dynamics, especially as it relates to children.

Crary, Elizabeth. *Pick Up your Socks . . . and Other Skills Grow-
    ing Children Need.* Seattle: Parenting Press, 1990. A unique
    workbook to help your child be accountable in many areas
    of life including household and school duties. For parents
    of children five years of age and up.

McCullough, Bonnie and Susan Monson. *401 Ways to Get Your Kids to Work at Home.* New York: St. Martin's Press, 1981. Making sure the kids learn to help.

Schofield, Deniece. "Confessions of a Happily Organized Family." *Cincinnati Writer's Digest,* 1947. A refreshing, no-nagging approach, with hundreds of practical ideas.

Of course, I highly recommend that most authoritative of all books on relationships, the Bible. Here the plumb line of thinking on the subject was given when we are told first to love God with all our heart, soul, strength, and mind, and second, to love others as ourselves. It doesn't get much better than that. To the extent that this book enables the reader to put these principles into practice, it has met its goal.

Need More Help?

If you would like a free introductory newsletter addressing the problems of MessieMates or information on support groups for MessieMates, how to obtain the books
suggested, and other helps available from Messies Anonymous, write to:

M-Anon
5025 S. W. 114th Avenue
Miami, Florida 33165